Stop Banging Your Head

Stop Banging Your Head

*Break Through
The Wall Of Frustration
In Small Business*

WILLIAM A. VAN HOY

Stop Banging Your Head

Published by: Value Marketing Systems LLC
PO Box 250
Achilles, VA 23001
support@valuemarketingsystems.com
www.ValueMarketingSystems.com
Get High Value Clients, a DBA of Value Marketing Systems, LLC

Book design by William Van Hoy
Cover design by Kenneth A. Van Hoy, KVH Creative

Printed by CreateSpace, An Amazon.com Company
Available from Amazon.com and other retail outlets

ISBN 978-0-578-16705-3

To my wife Barbara,
who watched me seclude myself for hours and waited
patiently for me to emerge. I owe you so much.

CONTENTS

ACKNOWLEDGMENTS

This book is the result of a lifetime of learning from mentors, associates, friends and family.

To Barbara Van Hoy, my wife, partner, foundation, and editor, without whose support both in business and in marriage, none of this would have been possible. I owe you so much more than I can ever repay.

To Sara Harris and Brian Harris for being my brainstorming focus group, and helping me shape my thoughts and direction.

To Marsha Campbell and Newell Campbell for being the greatest editors who made frank recommendations without fear of being brutally honest.

To Dick (Monty) Montgomery, my friend and novelist, who provided valuable counsel in how to write a book and showed me the way.

To Terry Conti, my friend and former coach, who inspired me to "big deal it" and think differently.

And, to all my friends who offered encouragement and support when they learned I was writing this book. At first I was reluctant to tell anyone, but once I did, without exception, they became cheerleaders and my support system.

Thank you all.

PREFACE

Years of sales training taught me that story telling is one of the best ways to get people to absorb and retain concepts. So in this book, I tell stories of three characters, Peter, Cathy, and Scott encountering walls of frustration in their businesses as things become complex and forward progress becomes difficult. They work hard with little additional success. Their stories are composites of multiple, real-life situations fused into three fictional characters, although they do not represent any particular individuals. The obstacles they face are universally encountered by small business owners in many industries. And I know that for a fact. But you may be asking yourself, are their obstacles applicable to me? Am I facing similar problems as theirs? Find out below. Read the following statements. See if any of them reflect your feelings.

- You feel frustrated with the difficulty of moving ahead in your business.

- You work long hours leaving little capacity to do more.
- You feel you should be doing better than you are even though you are putting in huge effort.
- You want to find a balance between business success and quality of life.
- You are searching for strategies to get you to the next level.

Do any of them fit you? If two or more of these statements are true for you then this book is for you. In the chapters that follow, you will find ideas and strategies to overcome obstacles holding you back and causing you frustration. When implemented they can make massive transformational impacts in your business life. Then you will discover the cherished balance between your work and personal life. Specifically, we are going to cover how to:

- Identify the obstacles holding you back and implement business solutions that will free you to move rapidly up to the next level.
- Realign the distribution of your workload so you can focus on creative elements of driving your business forward.
- Differentiate yourself so your best clients ask you to do more for them and your ideal prospects come to you asking for your service.

- Increase sales and profitability so you take home more while watching the value of the business grow.
- Achieve a balance between work commitments and your quality of life.

I will reveal all that I can in a limited number of pages. Before I conclude I promise to show you how to take it further. Why? Because that is part of my mission in life.

There is a book in all of us. For some, it takes a long time to find its way out. We have so much to say, so much to pass along, and so many lessons of life to share with others. For me this is an attempt to get some of it out.

Private sector business-life did not start for me until mid-life. I served twenty-one proud years in the US Navy as a surface warfare officer before embarking on a career as a financial advisor and business owner. Then after twenty-one years growing a business and advising clients, I moved along into a third career as consultant/coach for small business entrepreneurs.

For me, it is about what's next. I enjoy helping others, for that is part of my personal life mission. Like renowned sales trainer Zig Ziglar proclaimed, "You can have everything in life you want if you will just help enough other people get what they want."

Over the years I have seen people make the same mistakes over and over again. But, here is the thing. It is not the same people. Every new generation of entrepreneurs repeat the same mistakes. It takes many of them years to learn lessons that others learned before them. Worse than that, thousands of others fail to learn. So I wrote this book to talk directly to small business owners in hopes of positively changing lives, even for only a few.

I am reminded of the story about starfish. One morning as a man walked the beach, just as he had done many mornings before, he observed a young boy picking up objects and throwing them into the surf. As he approached, he asked the boy, "What are you doing?" The boy replied, "I'm throwing these starfish back into the water. They washed up in the last high tide. The hot sun will dry them out and they will die." The man said, "There are hundreds of starfish on this beach. How can you possibly make any difference?" As the young man threw another one back into the cool surf he replied, "I made a difference to that one."

That is my mission with this book, to make a positive difference in the lives of some small business owners who struggle to overcome the obstacles blocking their success. I will try to do that by telling stories. I hope readers will find nuggets of wisdom in these pages and apply them successfully in their own businesses.

INTRODUCTION

Five years he has been doing this, yet it seems much longer. Experiencing moderate success, he prospects, schedules meetings, gets commitment, analyzes cases, closes on solutions, and gets paid. Then he has to start all over again looking for the next one. It had been hard enough getting started with the first few, but now even this moderate volume is overwhelming. He can't do it all efficiently. On top of that he has to provide on-going service to existing clients.

The money is good, but he wants to grow to the next level. That's what they call it – the next level. That mythical place just above where he is now. Things are already complicated enough. He has no more time to give, he works sixty hours a week, and his wife complains she never sees him anymore.

How are the high producing veterans doing it? Not that all veterans do very well. It seems that many are just doing okay. But, a few are knocking the ball out of the park.

Those are the ones he wants to emulate, but how are they doing it?

Frustration is growing. It is like banging his head against a wall. He wants to break through, but it is not yielding. Something has to change – but how?

Does this sound familiar?

The Wall Of Frustration

His problem is the phenomenon I call the *Wall of Frustration*. It is that point in business where you get stuck at a certain level, nothing seems to work, it becomes increasingly difficult to move ahead, and frustration grows. Where do you go from here? What different strategies and tactics can you try? In the following chapters we will watch three business owners try new things to overcome the obstacles they face.

The Continuous Engagement Model

All businesses start with entrepreneurs selling products and services through a straight-forward customer sales cycle of prospecting, client conversion, and client service. Every business follows these three steps in one form or another.

I feel that the basic customer sales cycle (prospecting, conversion, and service) under-values the importance of regularly re-engaging with the clients. So I redefined the model to set an expectation from the very beginning that re-engagements are a valuable part of the relationship. The result is *The Continuous Engagement Model* with three steps: 1) Prospect Engagement; 2) Client Engagement; and 3) Planned Re-Engagement.

Planned Re-Engagement is the *power* step. From the outset, re-engagements are planned regularly to deliver additional real value. Taken one step further, the delivery uses *Type-V* service to blend perceived value with real value to build a premium service that warrants a recurring fee.

While each step is important, they all must be processed simultaneously in sufficient numbers to be a profitable business. Anything less is just a hobby.

Processing multiple business tasks is analogous to a stage performer spinning plates at the top of a rod. Place a plate at the top of the first rod and start it spinning. Then place a second plate on a second rod and start it spinning. Go back to the first plate to give it a couple of reinforcing spins. Then start a third plate spinning, but return to the previous plates to keep them spinning. And it goes on for the other plates.

This is what business owners must do with key business tasks. Like the spinning plates, they must continually make progress within each key task. It is hard to do when there is a lot of activity.

Successful professionals master the coordination to solve this problem, yet they are the minority. The majority have not done it. They reach a *Wall of Frustration*, stall, and stop growing.

This book describes the frustrations and struggles of three financial services professionals – Peter, Cathy, and Scott – each in a different phase of their career. All face their own *Wall of Frustration*. As the author, I interact with them, as consultant and mentor, to help them deal with issues; sometimes successfully and sometimes not.

I am qualified to do this because I have been there. I have encountered complexities, learned valuable lessons, and broke through to success. As a Certified Financial Planner, I ran a successful business practice with partners and employees for over twenty years before transitioning into consulting.

The Business Breakout Blueprint®

The lessons I learned during my career evolved into five fundamental business practices that worked well. I am going to share them with Peter, Cathy, and Scott. These practices are called *The Business Breakout Blueprint*®.

Practice #1 Build a team and delegate

Practice #2 Differentiate yourself with premium delivery

Practice #3 Stay in touch with prospects and clients

Practice #4 Boost recurring revenue with Type-V service

Practice #5 Prepare to transition while you are growing

These practices work independently or in combination with one another. They incorporate the critical principles within *The Continuous Engagement Model*.

I do not pretend that these are the only practices that work. Book stores are full of how-to, self-help books from experts describing other great ideas that work. I am a fan, I have read many of them. However, I do affirm this. The practices in *The Business Breakout Blueprint*® absolutely do work.

My sales leader years ago frequently said, "Anything will work as long as you do." He is right. I tried things, many things. Some were a waste of time and money, but I kept trying. Through evolution – not revolution – I settled upon the practices described in these pages as the best ones to use.

In this book I will tell stories in layers starting with revealing the *Walls of Frustration* obstructing Peter, Cathy, and Scott. Next I will describe how *The Continuous Engagement Model* works so we can introduce it to our characters. Then we will witness how they struggle applying the new strategies and see whether they are able to make them work. Following this we will examine the five business practices in *The Business Breakout Blueprint*®. Finally, we will address how you can pull it all together in your own business and move forward.

You may have reached a point in your own business where there is too much to do, not enough time to do it, or not enough people to get it done. You may be finding it difficult to see what has to be done to move ahead. By the end of the book, my hope is that you find powerful ideas to help you break through your own *Wall of Frustration*.

PART I

Hitting
The Wall
of Frustration

1

PETER'S STORY
THE QUEST

Peter approached me at the end of my presentation to the local chapter of financial services professionals. The program was "Better Advice with Premium Delivery." I enjoy speaking to these professional organizations, and this one had done its job for I was now talking with an interested prospect for consulting.

Smiling broadly Peter appeared to be in his late-40s or early-50s, slightly balding, wearing a gray classic fit suit, white shirt and patterned tie. He said, "I really liked your presentation about high value clients and fee-based planning."

He went on to say how he picked up some tips that possibly could help with the frustrations he is facing with his own business. He is in the insurance industry like many others in this group. After a bit more talking I said, "Why don't we meet next week for breakfast or over coffee and explore where you want to go with your business?"

"Sounds good," he replied, "Let's coordinate via email."

As it turned out, we met two weeks later at nine o'clock at Panera Bread. He ordered black coffee while I ordered coffee with Splenda plus a slice a banana nut bread (I love that stuff). The cafe was crowded at that hour so we sat at a two-top beside the window. Most of the people around us were talking business which created a constant background noise that let us have a private meeting in a crowded room.

We exchanged small talk, both understanding the importance of getting to know one another. There may be clues to suggest what motivates the other.

Peter is 55 years old, married to Stephanie, and has three adult children who live outside the house, two are married and one single.

For the past twenty-five years Peter has been an insurance agent with a nationally known insurance company and built a successful book of business with 825 clients. Actually most are really transactional customers, not clients, since they involve interactions to sell a product and last only long enough to complete the transaction. Conversely, the term "client" implies advisory relationships which are deeper relationships whereby the professional learns more about the person in order to deliver broader advice. Peter has this level of relationship with less than twenty percent of them.

He enjoys a comfortable living from his current level of production with the benefit of low overhead expenses made possible with an office in his house. The office has a separate entrance for clients. He has no employees and not sure he wants to change. His production level has been the same for two years. The problem is that he cannot break out and produce at a higher level.

Peter already works a full week and is unable to put in any more time. Most client meetings are at the customer's location which limits the number of meetings that can be scheduled. Since he does everything himself including scheduling meetings and processing business applications, he has little time to plan.

So I asked him the R-Factor Question™, a phrase coined by Dan Sullivan, a foremost expert on entrepreneurship and founder of *The Strategic Coach Program*®. I always lead a Discovery Conversation with the R-Factor Question™. "If we were meeting three years from today - and you were to look back over those three years - what has to have happened during that period for you to feel happy about your progress?"

He paused, his right hand wrapped around the bowl of the coffee cup while the left thumb and index finger stroked the cup handle, then said, "I'd like my production to be twice the current level by doing more planning and in a position to sell my practice in five to ten years."

"Sounds achievable. The other night at the chapter meeting you also mentioned getting into fee-based financial planning, charging a fee to do planning. Does it still fit in with what you just said?"

"Well, maybe. I'd like to see what it would take to get into it." He went on to state the hurdles to overcome to do fee-based financial planning in his company. He needs to get additional licenses and go through training.

"I could study and pass the Series-65 and Series-7 licensing exams, but it's a lot of work. So I'm uncertain whether to do it. I would also need an employee to help do the work. I don't have an employee now. I do all my own admin work. An employee would bring additional costs of salary and office space which I don't have in my home office. It may be hard to make that up?"

"Yes those costs are significant," I said. "Let's do some rough estimates. Out of your eight-hundred clients, twenty-five percent would probably be willing to pay for a comprehensive financial plan. Wouldn't you agree?"

"Yes probably."

"That is two hundred planning fees in the first couple of years. Then consider the additional production from implementing the recommendations from the plan such as commissions from larger insurance policies and other products. Industry studies show that implementation with a financial plan delivers forty percent higher production than cases without a plan. Plus, a big percentage of those planning clients would agree to pay a fee each year for ongoing advice. In the end, a fee-based financial advisory component in his practice would easily pay for the employee costs plus generate substantial additional net revenue."

"Yes I see what you are saying."

"Ongoing advisory fees would also add to the sales price of your practice when you get ready to sell. Buyers of a practice look at the amount of future predictable revenue from investment fees, insurance renewals, and financial advisory fees. You'll need to maximize those in your own practice in order to get a good price for your book of business."

"I had not thought about that."

We went on to explore this further. Then he settled into describing how his production has been the same for several years and how he is frustrated about it. After one half hour it was time to wrap up and pull it all together.

"Peter, You are stuck at a certain level of success having reached a barrier where it is difficult to move beyond. It's called the *Wall of Frustration*. You've stated that you meet with all clients at their location. Do you think you could have more selling opportunities if clients came to you?"

"Yes, I guess so."

"You also said that you do all of your own admin work. Do you think you would have more time to see more clients if you didn't have to do all the paperwork yourself?"

" Well, yes."

"Do you think the value of your business would be greater and buyers would pay more if recurring fees were maximized and came in on a predictable basis?"

"Sure."

"Do these things sound like an effective plan to you?"

"Yes."

"Would you like me to help you implement it?"

"Well that sounds good, but I'm not sure if I want to make all the changes necessary to make it happen." After some back and forth, we ended the meeting. He said, "Let me think this over and call you back in a couple of weeks."

Outside in the car I wondered if I had missed the signs. Was he a Do-It-Yourselfer just extracting some free information? Would he eventually want consulting help? Was he worth pursuing? Rule number one of consulting: *pursue only those that appreciate the value of your offering.*

Regarding paying for advice, there are three profiles of people: *Do-It-Yourselfers*, *Advice Receptive*, and *Advisor Dependent*. Do-It-Yourselfers almost never pay a fee for advice. They do research, gather information, then do it themselves. Advice-Receptive people are open-minded, frequently pay for advice, but still make their own decisions. Advisor-Dependent people need an advisor to give them direction. They generally see the value provided by a fee-based service. Clearly, Peter was not Advisor-Dependent. I initially thought he was Advice-Receptive, but maybe he isn't. Could he be a Do-It-Yourselfer? Who is he? Will he be willing to pay for consulting? We will see.

2

CATHY'S STORY
TRIAL BY FIRE

Cathy was full of frustrations when I met her three years ago at a monthly breakfast meeting of the Financial Planning Association (FPA). At these meetings, held in a typical hotel meeting room, people enter, grab a cup of coffee, and stand around networking while the buffet is set up. There is the normal small talk, "Hey, good to see you again, how's business?" or "How's the family?" After fifteen minutes, the financial advisors, attorneys, insurance agents, and mortgage brokers queue up for the buffet of scrambled eggs, bacon, and hash brown potatoes.

Cathy came to the table where I sat with four others and asked to sit. I indicated that the chair beside me was open, so she sat down. We ate and shared small talk among the six of us during the twenty minutes before the start of the main program. She deliberately sought me out and wanted to speak with me because she had heard me present a program to another organization.

At the end of the program, as everyone departed, Cathy asked if we could get together sometime outside the FPA meeting. I could tell she needed to talk so I said, "Sure, I've got thirty minutes to spare. Let's go over to the hotel coffee shop and talk there."

She was a third-year financial advisor and likeable, so I was pleased with the thought of being a mentor to her. It's in my DNA – I like helping others.

We walked across the hotel lobby to the restaurant where we sat and ordered coffee. We made small talk for five minutes. She was thirty-two years old. Bobby, her husband, was enjoying a good job in the city planning office. I did not know him well; only met him briefly one time at a business after-hours function. There are no children.

Our conversation came around to business. She was a practicing financial advisor for three years. Prior to that she had graduated from college with a B.A. History; then went to work in the marketing department of a health insurance company.

While attending a chamber of commerce educational workshop four years ago, Cathy met a woman her age who was a stockbroker and doing very well. Intrigued, she asked a lot of questions. She convinced herself that she could be a broker too. So she changed careers and sought a position as a financial advisor. After interviewing with several companies, she settled with a national company which offered good training and a strong diversified product line. They helped her get licensed for securities, insurance, and fee-based planning.

Cathy has been making steady progress in the last three years and earning an adequate income. But, she is not doing as well as she hoped, which is causing a lot of frustration.

I asked, "What are the main issues you're facing now?"

She told me that new business comes in peaks and valleys. She would launch a marketing campaign, bring in new prospects, meet with them, and start the financial planning process. Through case analysis she incorporated good financial strategies for investments and insurance. Then she would meet for the closing meeting, get most of the recommendations implemented, and end up with good production. Those were the peaks in income. Then she looked up and saw no new prospects in the pipeline. She would not get paid again until a new client was closed, which may be a couple of weeks. These were the valleys in income. Now she had to go out and start prospecting all over again. She said, "This is frustrating. I should be doing better than this. I tell myself to do more prospecting, but I'm already working nearly sixty hours a week. What am I doing wrong?"

Not surprising to hear this from a new advisor. Many young professionals run into this as their first *Wall of Frustration*. Things have gotten complex; too many things need to be done at the same time. That is one of the symptoms of *complexity paralysis*, working harder, but not making much progress. Cathy had reached that level. She was working long hours getting new business, yet not able to process them efficiently enough to move ahead. She was stuck at this level of success.

"You've reached the classic *Wall of Frustration*. Things have gotten so busy you don't have the capacity to do more without making some changes. What I mean is, you have to start automating and systematizing to improve production. There are two things you need to do. First, implement a system to stay in touch with prospects in the pipeline to motivate them toward making a buying decision. That will help relieve the need for new prospecting. It will keep some marketing momentum going while you are still working other cases. Second, hire someone to do the administrative processes for you. That frees you to focus on the critical money-making tasks. You need to do both things right now."

"I can't afford to hire someone now."

"Have faith, it will work and it will pay for itself in short order. It's like priming a water pump. You've got to put something in first before you get something out. A staff assistant will leverage your time. Hire someone part-time at first. You must start building a team now. It is really important and will pay off in no time."

In the early days of running a business most entrepreneurs want to do everything themselves because they have the time, but not the money. As the business grows, the entrepreneur still does the mechanics of operating the business, but devotes less time on creative entrepreneurship to grow the business. The fact that their business is moderately successful has created this situation.

When you reach this point it is time to bring in assistance to do the things that have to be done, but not done by you. Delegate. Free yourself to continue doing the critical things that must be done by you to make money and grow. *Build a team and delegate* is the number one practice in *The Business Breakout Blueprint®*.

I said, "You are probably spending a third of your time processing applications, running proposals, and other administrative work. Is that right?"

"At least."

"Well, instead of that you could be marketing and sitting in front of clients making money. Your time is valuable. In essence, you are paying yourself $75 to $100 per hour just to do administrative work. Delegate those things. Hire a competent person part-time to do those tasks at a much lower cost. Free up your time to do things that make money. The benefits will show up quickly. Building a team and delegating is more important than all the rest."

"May be I'll do the stay in touch system first and see where that takes me."

"Cathy, you can get more prospects and more clients, but you are still going to remain stuck unless you increase capacity. It is going to take a team to free you to do more and grow. That's what I did early on. An associate and I hired a high school intern to type, file, and make calls. It was the first step in freeing us to go out and make more sales. You should do the same now. Figure it out."

"Alright, I'll think about it. Tell me more about staying in touch with prospects. How does it work?"

Small businesses struggle with marketing, not because they fail to meet enough prospects, rather they do not adequately stay in touch with the ones they have already met. You see, not all prospects are ready to do business immediately. What happens to the ones that did not become clients right away? Most entrepreneurs get distracted and slowly lose touch with them. Isn't it a shame to lose touch. Eventually, when events change and those prospects are ready, they will do business with someone with whom they are familiar. It will be you if you have stayed in touch. That means staying visible in their lives, but not bothersome. Periodic visibility creates top of mind position. A good way of doing that is becoming a trusted resource through regular contact.

Set up a long term nurturing sequence with the goal of being a familiar, trusted resource. Touch people every week or two through a variety of channels such as email, Facebook, LinkedIn, direct mail, or other ways. For example, send them periodic emails with useful information on fascinating topics in "how-to" and "did-you-know" formats. Within each one include a call-to-action offer to learn more, then sometimes include an offer to do business. Avoid frequent, overt sales offers as that may be perceived as annoying. Keep prospects in this long-term sequence until they become clients or they ask to be removed. *"Stay in touch with prospects and clients"* is the third practice in *The Business Breakout Blueprint*®.

"Try to keep it simple at first. Send emails until you get the hang of it. Then add a Facebook business page, a LinkedIn profile, greeting cards, invitations to events, and other channels. The goal is to stay familiar, but not bothersome. And consider getting an assistant to help you do it."

"Hey, I can't afford anybody right now. I'll see what I can do by myself."

"Suit yourself, but I strongly recommend you find a way to build a team. You are going to remain stalled until you build capacity."

The server brought the check. We paid separately and said our goodbyes. "Let me know how things turn out and let's stay in touch," I said as we departed.

Cathy had been given two critical pieces of advice. I wondered if she would earnestly try to implement them.

3

SCOTT'S STORY
WE HAVE A PROBLEM

It was Saturday morning as I sat on the back porch reading the newspaper and drinking my first cup of coffee. The sky was a beautiful blue brought to life with a gentle breeze moving air in the low 70's. Our golf tee time was not until 11:30 AM so I had plenty of time to enjoy the moment. It was the beginning of an absolutely lovely weekend. Just then my iPhone rang. It was Jackson, a friend and colleague. "Have you heard? Robert suffered a major stroke last evening."

Robert is part of today's golf foursome with Jackson, Ted, and I. Robert and I have known one another for many years, but only began socializing the last five years. By socializing I mean playing golf occasionally. Plus we have met several times debating the best business models for a financial services practice. Robert is in his mid-50's, ten years younger than me and married to Jan for ten years. It is the second marriage for both. Each have adult children out of the home.

He is a successful financial advisor associated with a major financial services firm having been with them over twenty years. So successful in fact that he formed a team practice two years ago with Scott to help service his 510 client-groups.

Scott is a fairly junior advisor, in his mid-30's, who left a high school English teaching position three years ago to pursue an opportunity offering more growth potential. An opportunity that rewards his own efforts. That was an ambition he learned from his father. There was little opportunity for economic growth as a salaried teacher.

Scott joined the same financial services firm as Robert. The company helped him get licenses for investments, fee-based financial advice, and insurance. Compensation in the first year included a small draw-against-commissions plus all the additional commissions he could earn. In the second year and thereafter, it was commissions only. He did not realize how tough it was going to be getting started.

That is why he leaped at the opportunity to join Robert at the end of his first year. Robert needed an associate to help service his clients and approached Scott because of his tenacious work ethic. They split commissions on the joint accounts Scott services. These commissions offer potential for substantial growth, plus he can learn from a highly successful advisor. At the same time he continues pursuing his own clients. Scott likes that. It is a win-win.

They have individual offices within the company's branch office complex where eight other advisors also reside. One staff member, Maria, supports Robert and Scott. Maria is known to be extremely competent and the clients love her. All calls to the advisors go through Maria, so she knows everything that is going on allowing her to form great relationships with clients.

Scott likes the possibility of eventually buying out Robert's practice if things work out. However, he had not counted on this stroke. Neither of them did. Robert is never going to work again as a financial advisor. The partial paralysis and speech impairment will see to that.

As soon as he is declared totally disabled, the buy-out provisions of their group practice agreement kick in. They drew up the agreement two years ago as soon as they joined. It specifies that the acquiring advisor, Scott in this case, gets the accounts in exchange for quarterly installment payments to Robert over five years to pay off a promissory note equal to the value of the practice based on the level of recurring revenue.

The client relationships are owned by Robert, but the company has a strong interest in the new servicing advisor. The company's market group management will pay close attention to this transition. They will get involved to protect this big book of clients from poaching by outside advisors.

What was going to happen to Robert's practice? Scott remains relatively inexperienced. Can a junior advisor serve five hundred clients, many with large accounts? Will he be able to buy Robert out? Something needs to happen quickly, and Robert is in no shape to help.

It was two weeks after the stroke when Scott called me. He said, "I need some help. Robert has talked highly of you, so that's why I am calling."

The following morning we met in his office; I bumped a project to make room for the meeting. Their offices were on the second floor of a three story office building with ample parking out front and a two-acre duck pond in back serving as storm water drainage. It is well landscaped with a brick paver walkway all around. Scott's office, down the hall from the reception area, is rectangular with windows on the outside wall overlooking the pond. Entry to the office is through a solid wood door at the left end of the office paired with an eighteen inch wide, glazed side-light window. On the right end of the office is his executive L-shaped office desk facing the water through the outside window with the right-return work area along the right wall. A filing cabinet sat alongside the right return. At the left end of the office sits a 48 inch circular conference table with two chairs for clients. He will slide his low-backed executive chair over to the table when meeting with clients.

As we sat down at the circular table, Maria brought coffee just the way I liked it. She had recorded my preferences from a previous meeting, just as she did for clients. That was indicative of a professional attitude for client service.

I began, "Sorry for what is happening to Robert. I'll bet you are overwhelmed."

"You don't know the half of it. We have been reaching out to clients with calls and emails. Of course the top clients got personal calls from me. They all showed sympathy, but also want to know where we go from here.

"Company management says they want to help me, but they are really concerned the clients will leave for other brokers. So they want to get involved and communicate with clients too. I'm scared they may move some of the accounts to another advisor here. I don't want to let that happen, so I have to come up with a plan to address all this. I've got my own seventy clients plus Robert's five hundred clients to serve. Right now I am overwhelmed. What am I going to do?"

Scott has a big problem. He just got slammed into an unexpected *Wall of Frustration*.

Part II

Continuous Engagement And Type-V Service

4

THE CONTINUOUS
ENGAGEMENT MODEL

Before continuing with the stories of Peter, Cathy, and Scott, let's pause to examine the basic processes of selling and advising people.

The basic selling cycle is a natural process in business used by everyone in one form or another. It starts with attracting people, then selling a product or service, and then following up with service. The process is repeated over and over in an endless cycle.

The cycle becomes a *Wall of Frustration* when the volume gets overwhelming and the mechanics become complex. It stagnates into an inability to generate consistent leads, an inability to convert enough into sales, and an inability to deliver efficiently. These frustrations are happening to Peter, Cathy, and Scott as they fall victim to their own inefficiencies or complexities. Peter cannot raise his production from a large client base. Cathy cannot consistently get enough clients. Scott has too many new clients dumped on him at one time. What are they going to do? How are they going to rise above this? Should Peter and Cathy focus on getting new clients? Should Scott emphasize speed and efficiency seeing all the inherited clients?

Before answering these questions, let's review a reality that many forget. It is fundamental yet often overlooked. Doing more business with existing clients is far easier than selling to new prospects. Studies show the probability of selling to an existing customer is 60-70%, whereas the probability of selling to a new prospect is 5-20%. Therefore it is prudent to maximize sales to existing clients while selectively acquiring new clients.

That fact motivated me to rethink the processes in the selling cycle and emphasize <u>purposeful re-engagements</u>. That is, from the beginning, realign the whole process to focus on recurring engagements where additional value is delivered. Make re-engagements an intrinsic structural component. Make it a central part of what they are buying. I call this approach *The Continuous Engagement Model*, illustrated below in Figure 1.

Taken one step further, I call this *Type-V* service, where clients receive significant <u>value-added</u> services after the initial sale delivered periodically on a planned schedule. They <u>pay a recurring fee</u> for these value-added services.

The Continuous Engagement Model

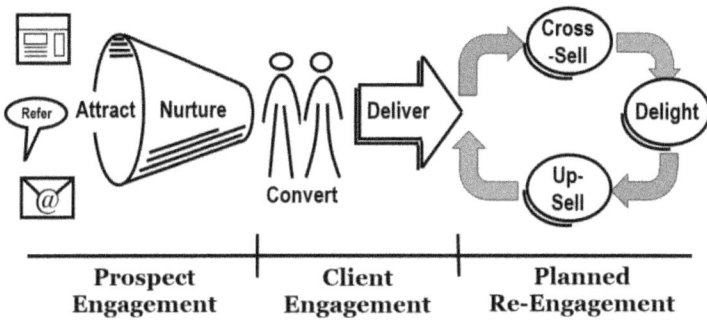

Figure 1

In this chapter, we will examine elements inside the Continuing Engagement Model to show how it differs from the traditional selling cycle model. After that we will re-visit Peter, Cathy, and Scott to see how incorporating Type-V service and the Continuous Engagement Model can help them.

While we are doing that, we will keep one thing in mind, this chapter is not intended to be a complete primer on prospecting, closing, or servicing.

5

PROSPECT ENGAGEMENT

Prospect engagement is the first step in the Continuous Engagement Model. It encompasses the spectrum of marketing for leads, qualifying prospects to match your ideal client profile, motivating them to take action, and nurturing the relationship of contacts not yet ready to buy. We can improve this step by tweaking a few things.

Define Your Target Market

The first tweak is defining your target market so you are focusing energy and resources on your ideal business prospects. These are specific groups of consumers at which you aim your products and services. They are the ones most likely to appreciate the value you have to offer. To avoid overlooking them, build a vivid profile of who they are. That profile guides your decisions for marketing campaigns, advertisements, seminars, social media, and others. Write it out. Describe the profile narrowly. You want to be able to close your eyes and see them. It may help if an existing client already perfectly matches your ideal profile. Describe that person.

The tendency is to be too general in hopes of encompassing a larger piece of the market. That is a mistake. Ultimately, an overly broad profile will cost you time, money, and energy. Do it right. Define your target profile narrowly. Below are some questions to help you visualize and refine the description of the ideal person.

Who Is Your Ideal Client?

- What are their biggest problems that you can solve?
- What are their likely goals and objectives?
- What are their demographics: age, gender, marital status?
- Where do they live? Is geography a factor for any reason?
- What do they do for a living?
- What is their financial situation – income, net worth, financial assets? This may be significant if you're offering relatively expensive items.
- What social or community affiliations do they have?
- What might motivate them to take action?
- What other aspects of their lives matter?

Consider High Value Clients

High Value Clients are people who appreciate greater value and pay more to get it. When presented two options, high value clients generally choose the one with greater value even at a higher price. They are found in all economic levels, and they do not have to be rich. High value clients are more *value-sensitive* than they are *price-sensitive*. They place great focus on customer service and less focus on mere price. Although price is important, it is not the controlling factor.

This in no way implies that price-sensitive people should be avoided. On the contrary, they are an important part of the market. Dealing with them requires slightly different emphasis than with High Value Clients.

The choice you make for a target market is actually going to be a reflection of who you are personally. If you are price-sensitive, then that naturally leads you to attract price-sensitive clients. Likewise, you will attract value-sensitive people if you are value-sensitive yourself. Either way it is okay. I am personally value-sensitive and thus it inspired my attraction to Type-V service.

If you offer products and services with large value components, then high value clients are a smart choice for you to pursue. Since they are less sensitive to price, you will not be under pressure to slash prices. On top of that, they will remain loyal as long as they continue receiving high quality service. High value clients are my personal favorite market.

Craft A Compelling 5-Second Message

When someone asks, "What do you do for a living?" How do you respond? You have only five seconds to get their attention, else the conversation is going to move on. If it works, you have another ten seconds to explain more.

Does five seconds or ten seconds seem short? Well it is not, it is sufficient time. Listen to TV and radio ads. They get lots of information across in a short time. Besides, the human attention span will not stay engaged longer than that, unless the message is extremely interesting.

I conducted some informal research on this when I was a sales leader. While having a conversation with a trainee, I surreptitiously held a stopwatch as I talked non-stop and looked for their body language to signal when they had enough and needed to speak themselves. Those signals were either grunts, shifts in body position, movements of hands, or saying "uh huh." Whichever it was, it signaled that they needed verbal relief. Typically it was fifteen to twenty seconds; the longest was thirty-five seconds. That was the signal for me to shut up and ask them any simple question so they could speak and relieve their internal pressure. That convinced me that people need frequent relief and you do not have much time to speak before turning it back to them. It applies to elevator speeches as well.

An "elevator speech," is the common name for the 5-second message. It is a brief, persuasive statement you use to spark interest in what you do. Your message should explain *how you help* people instead of just saying your job title. There is a big difference.

Imagine that you are creating a 5-second message to use at networking events when someone asks, "What do you do?" You could say, "I am a financial advisor." That is not very memorable. If fact, they will say okay then change the subject.

A better response would be something like this, "Everyone has financial goals, right? As a financial advisor, the people I work with rest easy knowing they are on track toward their goals and their money is invested wisely." That's much more interesting and shows the value that you provide to clients.

If you are asked to explain, or have the opportunity, use the longer 10-second version. Identify what makes you unique and your method of delivering value.

Suppose you are a business consultant, your two-part message might be like this. First five seconds: "We all work right? As a business consultant, my clients like to work every day and they make a lot of money doing it." Then, if the opportunity allows, say this: "I do three critical things for them. First, we identify obstacles holding them back so we can build strategies to overcome them. Second, we identify opportunities to quickly take advantage of. And third, I help them differentiate themselves so clients recognize their value. Are those the kinds of benefits you think business clients would find valuable? "

That last bit is a way to get them to internalize the message and to stay engaged.

These five and ten second messages are very important. Take time to write and practice them. You never know when you will need to speak them. Do not miss out during networking opportunities. Be prepared, have a well-honed message.

Here are some Do's and Don'ts:

- **Do** make your 5-second message sound conversational.
- **Do** make it memorable and sincere.
- **Do** leave the listener asking "So tell me more."
- **Do** consider including a compelling "hook" that will engage the listener and prompt them to ask questions.
- **Don't** let your speech sound canned.
- **Do** be ready for the unexpected.

When you get tired of it, simply rewrite it. I have rewritten mine over a dozen times.

You Are In This For The Long Term

Differentiate yourself from others. From the outset, let prospects know you are offering a long term relationship in which you will be delivering additional value through regular interactions with them. This is not a one-time transaction. Yours is a recurring, added-value relationship. That is why we call it *The Continuous Engagement Model*.

Prospect Engagement

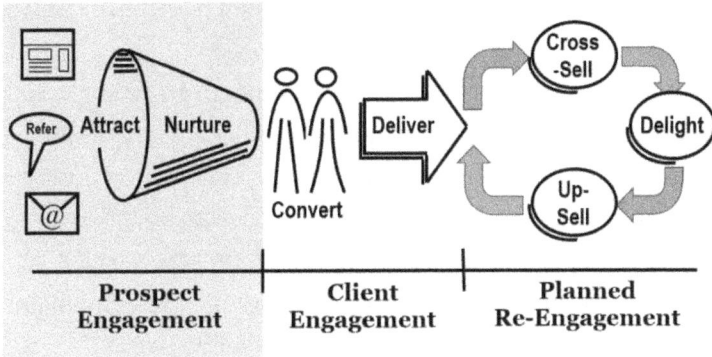

Figure 2

<u>Attract Qualified Prospects</u>

For most small business professionals, the ability to attract potential clients is the difference between growth and stagnation. There are many ways to do it, some are more productive than others, some are more cost effective. In the end, "anything will work as long as you do." Refer to Figure 2.

Of course, you want to attract prospects that are ready to buy, if that is possible. There are many ways to find prospects. Here are some sources that may work for you to find prospects.

Referrals. People whom existing clients and friends talked with and suggested they contact you.

Networks and Natural Market. People whom you see from time to time who may be interested in your service.

Seminars and Special Events. People whom show an interest in your service after hearing your presentation.

Website and Social Media Visitors. People who asked for more information via web entry forms on pages of your website and social media profiles.

Of course new clients may come from unexpected sources. I got one from a funeral. Rather, they called two weeks following the funeral of a special elderly client which I attended. The funeral service was attended by a hundred people; I was one of them. During the service, the officiant said, "The family wonders if their financial advisor would like to come up and say a few words?" They were talking to me – totally unexpected. So, I went up and shared a couple of fond anecdotes about Doris. The crowd liked it. Two weeks later a lady called saying she wanted to meet with me because she was impressed that a financial advisor cared that much about clients

Nurture The Relationship Until They Become Clients

Many prospects are not yet ready to buy. It may be that the timing is not right. Their circumstances may be changing. They are not comfortable making a decision tight now. Whatever the reason, they will say something like, "I've got to think about it."

That is okay, let them think about it. You have a plan for that. You are going to stay in touch.

Staying in touch is a matter of contacting people one way or another with an ongoing system. There are many ways to contact people and stay in touch. They do not have to be one-on-one meetings or phone calls. They could be emails, social media posts, greeting cards, direct mail, or a highway billboard for that matter. The point is to stay visible.

The next questions is how often do you touch someone? That depends. Successful professionals say more contact is better than less. Contacting high-value persons 24 times a year is a good standard. WAIT – that does not mean calling them 24 times—that is absurd! Nobody wants that much overt contact. No, it is more subtle than that. It means staying visible to them in a positive way as you deliver resourceful information. It is analogous to seeing your name, hearing about you, hearing from you, or another situation that reminds them of you in a positive way.

A Simple Follow-Up Approach That Is Not Pushy

Many professionals are vexed by the question of how to follow up without seeming too persistent or harassing. You want to stay top-of-mind, but you want to do it professionally.

For example, you talked with someone and they asked for more information. You sent it, but they have not responded. What do you do next? Send a second email saying, "I have not heard from you." No, try this instead.

Here is a simple technique that positions you as a valued resource rather than a pushy salesperson. After your first email, here is how you would professionally email again.

1. Go online to a website like Google News and Yahoo News.
2. Research a subject relevant to your prospect.
3. Find some article or story they might find interesting.
4. Email the link to them with a short message like, "I saw this and thought you might find it interesting."

That is it. You simply provide value and show them you are a trusted resource. Do this a couple of times and you show them you have been thinking about them. They probably will respond expressing their appreciation for your thoughtfulness. You have stayed on their positive side.

If all the foregoing works well, the prospects that are ready to buy will identify themselves, with your help of course.

6

CLIENT ENGAGEMENT

Client Engagement is the second phase of *The Continuous Engagement Model*. Refer to Figure 3. The prospects are motivated and ready to buy. What do you sell them? The answer is nothing—sell them nothing.

Instead, deliver solutions to their problems. You see, people buy solutions to problems, they do not buy products or services. They will pay for a product or service that solves their problem. With that in mind, identify the core problems faced by your target market. Then craft a message that positions your product/service as the solution. Basically it is finding their problem, then providing the "picks and shovels" to solve it.

Client Engagement

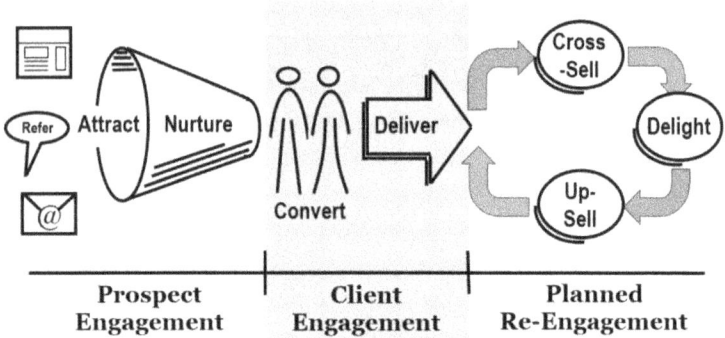

Figure 3

Take it one step further, make it a *Type-V* service. Build-in recurring engagements that happen periodically after the initial sale. At each of these engagements, deliver additional value. Then while delivering the additional value, look for opportunities for upsells and cross-sells. There will be many. If the additional value is compelling and the clients want to continue receiving it regularly, consider charging a recurring fee to deliver it. This is Type-V service where the "V" stands for value.

Let us put this into perspective by reviewing the four types of service delivery schemes.

Transactional sale. This is a one-off selling transaction of a product or service. Follow-up engagements for service may or may not occur.

Subscription service. This is a recurring, paid membership allowing the buyer access to benefits whenever they choose.

Retainer service. This is a pre-paid agreement allowing the buyer to <u>request and receive</u> benefits at a time of their choosing.

Type-V service. This is pre-paid access to recurring, value-added services that are <u>pre-planned</u>. The buyer knows what they will get and when they will get it. The clients pay a recurring fee to be part of the service.

Offer Type-V service regardless of the type of business you are in. Give customers a choice. Offer them an option of a basic service for a one-time fee, or a Type-V service with a recurring fee. Consider heavily promoting the Type-V service offering as your premium option with the best overall value.

I offered a Type-V service when I was actively practicing as a financial advisor. Clients paid an annual fee in return for receiving on-going, written, and actionable financial advice delivered during four theme-based meetings each year.

Successfully Engaging Clients

Structure your options to appeal to their sensitivity whether price-sensitive or value-sensitive. Adjust the features and benefits accordingly. Make it easy for them to see how you are helping them solve their problem.

7

PLANNED RE-ENGAGEMENT

Planned re-engagement is the *power step* in the Continuous Engagement Model. It is a structured plan for future engagements based upon specific periodicity or triggering events. It is an integral part of the promise. Clients pay a fee at the beginning and again on a recurring basis. It differs from the traditional transaction model where service is an add-on, an after-thought, and may not even happen. Refer to Figure 4 below.

This is not a new model. Some businesses use it as their standard. For example, business coaches have regular meetings with clients who pay them regularly. Social media managers make regular posts for clients and get paid. It is similar, but slightly different than businesses delivering repetitive services such as lawn service, LP gas/heating oil delivery, or dentists. They get paid for specific products and services as they deliver.

Planned Re-Engagement

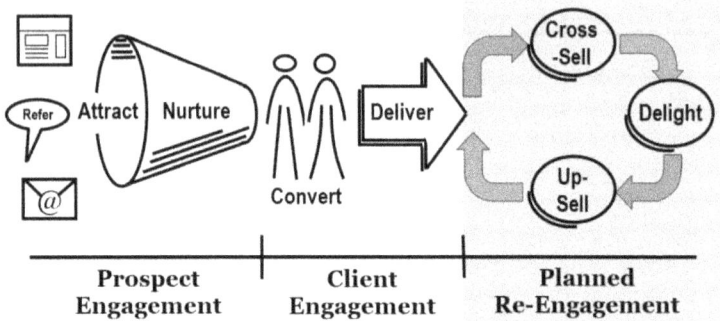

Figure 4

Some other businesses have not yet seized the opportunity to create planned re-engagements and charge for them. Those are the ones this book can help. There is a huge revenue opportunity waiting. All it takes is converting existing services into recurring engagements, then charging for that.

Type-V Service And Pricing

Consider making the re-engagement system a Type-V service where the clients are buying into future interactions which will continue bringing them value. They will pay a recurring fee for access to this higher level.

Type-V services have higher fees than one-time transactional services. With Type-V, clients buy multiple, future deliveries of additional value covered by an initial fee. Thereafter, if the recurring value is worthy, they will happily continue paying.

Create The Opportunity For Upsells And Cross-sells

Existing customers are likely to buy more products and services when they are relevant to things they initially purchased. That is why these re-engagement opportunities result in high revenue growth.

Look what your customers previously purchased and offer them additional products/services that make sense. While doing this continue delighting them with extraordinary service. Planned re-engagement is the door to exponential growth. This is the most powerful step in the model.

Now let's get back to Peter, Cathy, and Scott.

PART III

Hitting The Wall
More Than Once

8

PETER
ROUGH ROAD AHEAD

Three weeks passed following our meeting at Panera Bread, while Peter and I exchanged five emails. He was fishing for more specifics about what to do. I responded with useful answers, giving him just enough information to be helpful, yet not enough for him to do it all himself. His fifth email expressed a realization that he needs a coach to help change things if he is to move beyond his current level. I responded with a suggestion to meet again; he agreed.

Starbucks is one of seven stores along the right leg of the horseshoe-shaped Hilltop North Shopping Center. It was sandwiched between the wireless phone store on the left and the liquor store on the right. Out front in the sidewalk area, five people sat in the two groups at the wrought-iron tables.

Inside I found Peter seated at a table with a Venti size coffee by his right hand and a notepad and pen by his left. It was 9:55 AM, our appointment was at ten. This was a good sign, he was anxious to get going. I greeted him, laid down my black portfolio and iPad, then moved to the counter where I ordered the usual Grande vanilla latte and a slice of banana walnut bread.

Upon returning I said, "Good to see you again. How is Stephanie?" referencing a comment in his last email that his wife was not feeling well.

"Oh, she's fine now. Went to the doctor's office and got some antibiotics. The bug went away in two days, and now she's fine."

"Good to hear. You ready to get started?"

"I am, but first let's settle on the things you're offering to do. How long it's going to take and what it's going to cost?"

He is direct, I like that.

"Sure thing. Let's clarify where you are now and compare that with where you want to be."

"Alright."

"You've stated you want to double your production in the next three years, you may or may not want to do fee-based financial planning, and you want to be in a position to sell your practice in five to ten years. Is that correct?"

"Yes, essentially it is. I've decided not to get licensed to do fee-based financial planning, but doubling my production and getting ready to sell are still true."

"Alright, let's take it from there. Here's what I recommend. We need to do three things. The first thing is improve the efficiency of how you meet with clients so you have more interactions and more selling opportunities. We will start with your A-level clients that you are going to identify through a categorization exercise."

"Okay."

"Second, we will redefine how you approach client meetings. You are going to focus more on delivering financial advice rather than just servicing products. That will warm them up and open them up for bigger opportunities."

"What's the third?"

"The third thing is examining the factors that determine the fair market value of a financial services practice. We need to improve your most important factors in order to maximize the value of your practice in preparation for selling whenever the time comes. Sound good?"

"Yeah, um, all right, go ahead," he said in a slow pace that revealed some apprehension.

I lost focus as a young man bumped my chair from behind. He squeezed through the narrow gap to get to the table against the wall where the pretty brunette sat reading her iPad. She was scrolling frequently, so she must be viewing a social media site and not text-heavy email content. She looked up in surprise, smiled broadly, and motioned for him to sit down.

Regaining my focus, I continued. "This will take you two months to get up and running and start seeing good results. At some point in time you're going to need an assistant to help out, but we'll address that later. Right now let's focus on first things first, making more money."

I told him the fee. He wasn't surprised as it was the same as I told him before. He signed the service agreement and paid with his American Express card which I swiped through the Magtek card reader plugged into the iPad. The payment went straight into my business bank account. I punched in his email address to send the receipt.

"I'm glad you take American Express, I like the membership rewards points. Some vendors don't take it because the transaction fees are higher than MasterCard."

"Yes I've heard that too, but a business person needs to make it easy for people to do business with them. All they have to do is build that small additional cost into the price they charge. Not doing so is short-sighted and makes them look bad. I've witnessed it personally. A couple of years ago I invited a wealthy client and his friend to join me for lunch at the Harbor Club. You know, the fancy lunch-dinner club atop the bank building downtown. They each insisted on paying their own bill. My client offered the waiter his American Express Card and was told they didn't accept it, only Visa, MasterCard, or Discover. When the server walked away, I asked him what he thought about that. He said he thought they were cheap. The management was not making it easy for him to do business with them. So he is not coming back. That made a memorable impact on me. Make it easy for people to do business with you."

Getting back on point I said, "Ok, so I'll put together a plan of action with milestones. We will get together in your office to go over it and get started. How does next Wednesday look? We will need two and a half hours."

We are off to a good start. Let's see how he follows through. Is he willing to make the effort and sacrifices necessary to make the change?

It has been said that people are ready, willing and able. Many are able, some are ready, yet few are willing to make the changes necessary to break through the *Wall of Frustration*. I wondered if Peter is truly willing to make necessary changes.

Wednesday arrived. My homework was done and I was ready to meet with Peter. His home is in an upscale community of white-collar professionals. It is a large brick veneer, two-story colonial style house with two car front-loading garage on the left. It sits on a one acre lot well landscaped in front and tall pine trees in the backyard bordering the eighth hole of a golf course. I have played here before.

His lot is on the left side of the eighth hole. It is a long par five with a right dog-leg away from his house just at the location of his lot. It gives a beautiful long axial view down the remainder of the fairway toward the well bunkered green. It is the number six handicap hole on the course as a result of the fairway bunker on the left near the turn, the huge oak tree on the right guarding the inside bend of the dogleg, and the three sand traps guarding two sides of the green.

Peter's office is in the large room above the garage. A sidewalk on the left end of the house runs from the driveway to the side entrance that accesses an enclosed stairway to the second floor office. An attractive shingle sign at the outside door establishes the location of his office.

The office is a twenty by twenty foot space organized into three functional areas. One is anchored by his large oak desk, another is a lounging space with a two-person sofa, side chairs on either end separated by small tables with lamps, and a third space along the back with filing cabinets.

There is no small conference table for client meetings as I had hoped. It seems that he will conduct business across his large desk whenever he meets clients here. Was that the way we were going to meet today? To my pleasant surprise, he came around to my side of the desk and sat in one of the side chairs, I took the other.

Just then the door to the second floor living area opened. Stephanie walked in carrying a tray with a stainless steel carafe of coffee, two cups and a bowl of sweeteners. She said, "I heard you're going to be here, so I thought you would enjoy some coffee." She was right. She placed the tray on the desk at the side nearest to us. "Peter has been talking about this meeting for two days now. Hope it works out." Then she was gone as quickly as she had entered.

"Let's begin at the end," I said. "Let's talk about the important elements of valuing a financial services practice so we can understand the things you need to do to structure your business properly. That will make our plan of action more sensible."

Our discussion began with how to value a financial services practice and the fundamental question of who owns the client-relationship. Typically an independent financial advisor owns the relationship and thus can sell it as equity. On the other hand, an advisor affiliated with a large company has only rights to the stream of on-going commissions and the right to transfer to another by way of split commissions. The company owns the relationship.

Consider the first arrangement where the advisor owns the relationship and thus has equity. The sale can be simple or complex depending on the size of the practice, the nature of the practice (consultative versus transactional), fees or commissions, investment management or insurance, individual securities or managed funds, or a combination of these. Then there are physical assets such as furniture, equipment, and real estate. Also personnel issues such as associates and employees affect valuation considerations.

Consider the nature of the relationship. Does the advisor meet with clients on a regular basis and have "sticky" relationships endearing them to the practice? Or are they transactional customers who may easily move to another advisor? Do they pay a fee for ongoing advice?

All these affect the perception of how much a buyer will offer to a seller. That perception boils down to four factors:

1. Amount of on-going income,
2. Likely persistence of the income stream,
3. Likely opportunity for new business, and
4. Physical assets.

The biggest of these four factors is #1 the amount of on-going income. That is followed by #2 the "likely persistence of the income." The least factor generally is #4 the physical assets. Factor #3 "likely opportunity for new business," is a reflection of the quality of the client base and is used as a weighting factor to adjust, up or down, the value determined by factors 1 and 2.

In essence, factors 1, 2, and 3 are measurements of relationships with the clients – the Book of Business. The sale really being the transfer of client relationships. Will they transfer? How many will transfer? How long will they stay? A practice with deep relationships will experience high transfer rates to the new advisor, whereas transactional relationships experience lower transfer rates. If the Book of Business contains assets and services that pay on-going fees, how many years will the fees stay before they defect?

These are the considerations for selling a practice with equity. This is generally the case with independent financial advisors and groups of advisors.

On the other hand, consider the arrangement where the advisor has no equity ownership, the company owns the relationships, and the advisor is entitled only to the income stream. This is true with many large companies. The company generally has prescribed guidelines of how the income and client relationships are transferred from one advisor to another.

For example, a major financial services company may allow a transfer over three to five years dependent on the size of the practice. The mechanism is a split-commission arrangement. In year one the seller retains a high percentage, while the buyer gets a minority percentage even as the buyer is doing all the servicing. Then over the prescribed period of time, the percentages shift annually with the buyer getting more and the seller less. In the end, all the on-going commissions accrue to the buyer. If clients leave during the transition period the on-going commissions naturally cease. These splits apply to existing products. If new products are sold, the commissions accrue to the new advisor. This describes Peter's situation. He will have to sell via a split-commission arrangement to another advisor within the company. He is not allowed to sell to advisors affiliated with other companies.

I concluded this explanation by saying, "As you can see, we need to deepen relationships with clients and make them more 'sticky.' Plus we need to identify how to increase recurring revenue from products. We want to build your stream of on-going revenue. Any questions?"

"No."

Next we moved into how to restructure his client service model to develop 'sticky' relationships. In the past he has been seeing clients inconsistently, only when a need arises. It was a reactive arrangement that left clients without a clear expectation of what was next. It did not draw clients into a deeper relationship.

Three-fourths of his 825 clients owned insurance products. They were transactional relationships and not consultative relationships that generate deep ties. I wanted him to transition into consultative relationships which lead to fast-growing, profitable practices. That is the way to go to make more sales.

I was recommending to Peter to shift towards the consultative approach. Admittedly he cannot offer fee-based planning now as a stand-alone service because he does not have the appropriate license. Nor could he have the cost of financial planning advice covered by investment fees tied to a percentage of assets as many financial advisors do.

That type arrangement may be modified in the future by changes in the definition of a *fiduciary* in guidelines issued by the Department of Labor under the Employee Retirement Income Security Act (ERISA). These changes may have profound implications.

I am suggesting to Peter to offer general financial advice not covered by a fee. It is not the arrangement I prefer, but it will have to do.

A financial planning relationship lets clients know they have a long-term relationship with a trusted resource. It gives them comfort knowing what comes next. That is the consultative arrangement I want Peter to get into with his clients.

I presented a client service model where he meets with them one or two times a year dependent upon how they are categorized. That will be the first activity to go through the entire client list and label them as A-level, B-level, or C-level. The A-level clients are those with the biggest accounts, those who invest regularly, present the biggest growth opportunity, and make the most referrals (Champions). B-level clients are the middle area and offer possibility of moving up to the A-level. C-level are those demonstrating the least likelihood of moving up, and not investing regularly, and generally have the smallest account sizes. He should begin this categorization audit right away. This categorization arrangement is commonly used in various forms by many service professionals. I recommended it to Peter because it works.

We talked about shaping his client service model to be unique. We will structure it to deliver on-going service, pre-planned re-engagements, and opportunities to up-sell/cross-sell products. A well designed client service model builds strong relations with clients and delivers on the value proposition.

There are all sorts of designs for service. Most are straight-forward and simple. I prefer arrangements that are unusual, creative, and display perceived value. I want the client to feel they are getting something unique, not available from other advisors. I am recommending a simple version to Peter to get started.

Perceived value is a complement to real value and just as important. Its importance is underestimated by most people. Yet it raises the level of satisfaction enjoyed by clients. We will add several perceived value features to Peter's model. I suggested he consider naming his model *The Economic Growth Program*. It will have three levels of relationship named *Consultative*, *Advisory*, and *Standard*.

In the <u>Consultative level</u>, he will meet clients face-to-face two times per year for financial planning advice and account review. They will meet preferably in his office as much as possible or at their location if necessary. He will do this for A-level clients.

In the <u>Advisory level</u>, he will meet clients once each year, face-to-face for general planning advice and account review. They could meet more often as necessary. They will meet in his office only. He will do this for B-level clients.

In the <u>Standard level</u> , reserved for C-level clients, he will meet only in his office for review of their accounts. He will offer additional financial advice when they display interest in growing.

I prefer that he meet more often with clients, but he has too many to make that practical.

In a further effort to make it unique, we will change the name of "meetings" to "Assessments." The term review meetings will no longer be used. Each Assessment will have a unique theme such as Investment Assessment, Protection Assessment, etc. I have found that clients look forward to theme-based engagements, while resistant to simple review meetings. They recognize that something specific will be discussed at theme-based engagements and their level of expectation is higher.

Give them something of value to take away from the Assessment. Create an attractive package that summarizes the agenda, identifies critical issues, spells out actionable recommendations, and account summaries. It should look professionally polished. Its appearance conveys the importance the advisor places upon the Assessment thus heightening the perceived value. Do it for Consultative and Advisory engagements.

Peter will have to go through a rigorous startup period while he organizes his contact management system and schedules appointments several weeks in advance. Once past the startup, it will be much easier as he runs the system consistently and efficiently. Scheduling and preparation will be done in advance. At the Assessments, clients will recognize that greater value is being offered, they will respond with more business, and offer better referrals.

At this point Peter holds up his hands and says, "That's a lot of work. I'm busy enough as it is. I don't see how I'm going to get it all done."

"I agree with you that it is a lot of work. You have to start somewhere and you have to start sometime or else you're never going to move ahead. It will be easier if you have assistance. Can you get a part-time assistant? An assistant is going to make all the difference in the world. Maybe Stephanie can help out for a while?"

"All right, I'll work it out somehow, but geez!"

He did not expect to have to change so much. Peter probably envisioned only some minor tweaks to his process, not this major change I am proposing. His words and actions are demonstrating he falls on the right end of the *20-50-30 Change Scale*, where 20% welcome change, 50% are neutral fence-sitters, and 30% resist change.

"Okay Peter, let's end the meeting here with this thought. Let's focus on your objective. Within three years you want to double your production. You've convinced me that you have hit a wall and find yourself unable to generate at a higher level. You are maxed out on time. You're running hard just to maintain pace with where you are. Is that right?"

"Yeah."

"Well if you keep doing what you've always done, you'll keep getting what you've always gotten. You've got to change. Change is hard. Our human physiology subconsciously identifies change as danger and sends out alarm signals telling us to avoid change. We need to overcome that emotion by replacing it with a positive emotion linked to a pleasurable gain. We will do that by focusing on a worthwhile goal that is achievable. Your mind will find a way to do whatever needs to be done to get nearer that worthwhile goal." I paused to let that sink in.

"So Peter, let's define some interim milestones that lead to your goal. Get started now on the A-B-C categorization and identifying your best clients. Also look at your Book of Business report to see which clients hold products that should be repositioned to ones with small, on-going fees. I'll call you in two weeks for our regular teleconference. Depending on where you are, we will proceed to the next steps of establishing the new client service model. Can you do that?"

"Yes I can do that."

Driving away I kept thinking, "He is *able* to change. He says he is *ready* to change. But, is he really *willing* to put in the necessary effort to change?"

9

CATHY
REVOLUTION OR
EVOLUTION

I call it the "Revolution Deception" – the myth that revolutionizing your business always leads to breakthrough success. It does not. In fact, revolution can lead to crippling stagnation. Most of the time, rapid revolutionary changes lead to dysfunctional paralysis in business. For most people, gradual change is better. That is the approach I am taking mentoring Cathy.

Over a period of three months I saw her two other times at FPA meetings where we exchanged brief chats, but nothing in depth. She did share that she implemented the stay in touch emails and it seemed to be working out.

Another month passed. Then I saw her at an awards luncheon for non-profit organizations. It turns out she is actively involved with a group advocating Chesapeake Bay clean water, while I serve on the board of directors of a group providing temporary shelter and counseling for at-risk young people. We talked during the networking period before the lunch.

Cathy was excited to recount a story about a new client. An old referral called her and said he needed to meet soon. Cathy had met the man two years earlier, however at that time he was not ready to start financial planning. Now he wanted a meeting right away. So they met without the wife present. Right away the man told her the urgency for the meeting. He was dying of cancer. The doctors said he had only a couple months left. He wanted Cathy to help get things straight and take care of his wife. He called Cathy because she was the only advisor staying in touch with him. Another broker associated with his company's 401(k) retirement plan never kept in touch. He had to call the broker whenever he needed something. Now he wanted someone proactive.

The doctor's prognosis was off by two weeks, the new client died in six weeks not eight. Fortunately by that time Cathy had completed the financial analysis and designed a strategy.

The client passed away leaving two relatively large life insurance policies, a moderately large 401(k) plan, and other securities. The wife was going to be well taken care of. This was a big case albeit a sad one. This one instance proved to Cathy the value staying in touch.

Cathy went on to say she is building a team. She arranged for part-time staff support by paying the front desk receptionist for a few hours a week. That is permissible because the receptionist (Shirley) is working for the company only part-time. Now she helps Cathy schedule appointments and sends out emails in the stay-in-touch campaign. All that is helpful, yet Cathy is still feeling overwhelmed. She put a lot of time into this case.

I asked how much she charged as a planning fee. She said, "not enough."

"Why not?"

"Well, I don't think our financial plan is good enough."

"You mean your advice is substandard?"

"No, no, it's not that. I think I give good advice. It's just that the whole thing looks just boilerplate."

I was not surprised to hear this. As a matter of fact that's what many advisors say. A couple of years ago, while conducting a half-day workshop for another financial services company, I took an informal poll. The workshop was "Acquiring High Value Clients." I asked the eighteen advisors in attendance why their fees were not higher at a level they deserved. The most popular answers were (1) they were not proud of the level of service they offered and (2) they were not proud of how the financial analysis document appeared to clients. Upon further probing, they universally felt their quality of advice was good, but in their opinion, it did not appear good to the clients. That was their opinion not the opinion of their clients.

We examined it further as a group. It was agreed they invest twelve to sixteen hours on each case including meeting time, case analysis, preparation, and presentation.

Their effective hourly compensation was too low compared to the critical, transformational value they delivered to the clients. They deserved better compensation.

So I told them about changing the way they deliver advice. Reframe the interaction so it is perceived as more valuable. Modify their process and the deliverable to look, sound, and feel more upscale. The clients will respond. Most advisors underestimate the importance of perceived value. They should use perceived value to highlight the difference between them and other advisors. You see, *it is not enough to be the best at what you do, rather it is being the only one who delivers it the way you do.*

Clients are used to the standard way of receiving financial advice, meeting with advisors once or twice a year to review accounts. They meet around a table, look at account statements, review hypothetical projections, and listen to verbal recommendations. That is the standard model used by many advisors. It is simple and it works. Remember, anything will work as long as you do.

Some clients find this model satisfactory. These clients are focused primarily on results and less sensitive to perceived value. So for them, continue delivering their review meetings in the traditional way.

Other clients may respond to a different approach. Consider a model that deepens the client-advisor relationship with more in-depth focus on key financial issues? Conduct meetings that focus narrowly on specific things at each meeting. Consider theme based meetings focusing on different subject areas. For example, one meeting could update important portions of the financial analysis plus review investment accounts. Another meeting could review estate planning and protection planning as well as review investment accounts. Still another meeting could review tax related issues to identify end-of-year actions to save taxes.

Give these meetings unique names that makes them sound important. For instance, call them "Assessments" not "meetings." Create printed deliverables packages with the agenda, observations, list of critical issues, and actionable recommendations. Make the deliverable look professional. Clients will recognize clear value in the recommendations and perceive them as more authoritative. Every year thereafter, deliver additional written, actionable advice. Then consider charging an annual fee, not just a one-time fee. This is Type-V service – more value delivered in a unique way.

Take it one step further and make the presentation in a unique way. People respond to special treatment by placing greater value on it. One way that works is treating them like important executives being briefed by an expert advisor in a boardroom setting. Here is how to do it. Meet with clients in your office around a conference table. Present the meeting using a PowerPoint presentation shown from a wall-mounted display. It throws off the vibe of a high level executive briefing of great importance. Within the PowerPoint slides show observations, critical issues, and actionable recommendations. Keep it simple and to the point. Provide a copy of the slides bound in a professional way. Clients will use it to take notes and take home for reference. They come away feeling like they dealt with an expert.

Special treatment motivates clients to implement a high percentage of recommendations. This is possible by way of reframing how you deliver the service. Reframing is the essence of Type-V service. The second practice in *The Business Breakout Blueprint®* is *differentiate yourself with premium delivery*.

I was telling this to Cathy the same way I told it to the eighteen advisors at the "Acquiring High Value Clients" workshop. Just then, the announcement came through the overhead speakers instructing us to proceed to the ballroom where lunch is being served for this gathering of non-profit professionals. As we walked to our assigned seats at separate tables, Cathy asked, "Can we get together at your office?"

"Sure, Wednesday the fourteenth works for me, how about you?"

"That's good. I'll confirm via email."

I am glad Cathy is making progress and seems to have broken through the first *Wall of Frustration* by staying in touch and building a team. Is she moving gradually enough or does this feel like revolutionary change?

Soon she will meet a fork in the road and choose between the standard service-on-demand transactional model, or the Type-V Planned Re-Engagement model. Which will she choose and have the capacity for?

10

SCOTT
PROBLEM SOLVED
OR IS IT?

In the blink of an eye our whole world can change. And so it had for Robert and Scott. Now Scott and I sit at the small circular conference table in his office separated by the statement that he is overwhelmed and is on the verge of panic. It has been two weeks since Robert's stroke and one day after Scott called saying "I need some help."

This is my cue for the Discovery Conversation. "If we were meeting three years from today - and you were to look back over those three years - what has to have happened during that period for you to feel happy about your progress?"

"Three years! Wow, I just want to get through the next month. I've got five hundred client groups to get friendly with. It's hard to look into the future."

"I hear you, that's got to be tough. Let's try to focus. In three years, where do you hope to be?"

"In three years I want to have all our current clients staying with us. I want to be making enough to comfortably afford the buy-out from Robert. We have a five year buyout agreement you know. Plus I want to be on pace to earn more than Robert. Is that specific enough?"

"Yes it is a good start. You certainly have a unique situation here which is good and bad. It's bad because of Robert's condition. It's good because it offers an opportunity to put your own brand on the business with the cooperation of your clients. Here's what I mean."

I continue, "Robert and I talked about his practice from time to time. As a matter of fact, we've had some lively debates. He accumulated a large amount of assets under management and the clients love him. But, he was missing the boat on recurring revenue. That is why he has been gradually transitioning from a commissioned mutual fund model to a fee-based investment management model, but he did not do many comprehensive financial plans. Instead he was bundling financial advisory fees with investment management fees. I suggested separating them to draw a clear distinction to the value of financial advice. He and I talked about it, yet he was resistant to change. Too bad though, a tremendous growth opportunity lies there."

"I'm not anxious to take on more change right now. I've got my hands full."

"You certainly do. However, your current situation is changing anyway regardless of what I suggest. Might as well sculpt it to be most beneficial for you. I'm talking about continuing the transition to fee-based investment management just as he was doing. Plus, differentiate the fees on financial advice from fees on investment management. You may be forced to do that anyway due to changes in the ERISA definition of fiduciary relationship. You are already doing fee-based comprehensive financial planning with your own clients so why not do it for the new clients as well?"

"Sounds reasonable."

"Let's you and I define a service model for new clients to position fee-based financial advice separately from fee-based investment management. We will make it a big deal to highlight the importance. First, we will communicate it to clients with a series of communications informing them about this enhanced client service program. That will keep them satisfied while you meet and gradually implement the program. We will use a combination of phone calls, emails and letters to reach them."

"Okay."

"As that gets started, you and I will finalize a design for service where clients choose between levels of service. The top level of service will deliver comprehensive financial advice plus investment management. You'll meet with these clients three times a year. Their annual financial advisory fee will be separate from the investment management fee. You will have that conversation with them when you meet next."

"I will need help defining how to tell them."

"Alright. The second level of service will deliver investment management only. You will meet with these clients once per year or more often as necessary. In both levels you will switch investments to fee-based versus commission based just as Robert has been doing."

"Why would the top level pay more for financial advice?"

"Scott, there is a fundamental principle here: *no more free advice*. You are going to show them how your new client service system is better and delivers more value. Your new comprehensive advice program will be more than just account reviews – much more. You are going to have meetings centered upon themes that deal with all the areas of financial planning like retirement planning, protection planning, tax planning, estate planning, and investment management. At each meeting you are going to give an overview of where they are now, identify critical issues, and then provide written, actionable advice on what to do next. You are going to help them get their arms around all their financial issues. Believe me they will love it. I did it for my clients."

"You did that? How did that work out?" he said while taking notes.

"Worked out extremely well. Your clients, just like my former clients, will pay you an annual fee for the comprehensive advice. You will set it up so they pay automatically with a deduction from their money market account. That makes is easy on you and them. You won't have to ask for a check every year and they won't have to agonize over writing a big check. No one likes to write checks. The revenue from those fees will come to you every year like clockwork, and it will grow to be substantial."

He looked up, "Keep going, I'm taking notes."

"Essentially we are implementing components of a business model I developed with five key business practices. I call it *The Business Breakout Blueprint*®. We are going to implement some of those practices in your business, but we are going to do it gradually." I went on to describe the five practices.

1. Build a team and delegate. Install systematic processes to get more things done with less effort.
2. Differentiate yourself from others with premium delivery by being the only one who delivers services the way you do.
3. Stay in touch with prospects and clients to nurture warm relationships and to motivate them to do business with you.
4. Boost recurring revenue using Type-V service that pay on-going renewal fees.
5. Prepare to transition your practice even while you are still growing by maximizing the things that affect the value of the practice.

"We are going to gradually roll out the first four practices for you. We will start right away with staying in touch with clients with a short-term campaign. Then move on to differentiating you from others with the enhanced client service system and fee-based financial planning. I have a ready-made program package we can install. Once we are convinced we have those working, we will gradually promote strategies for recurring revenue as you meet with the clients."

"Sounds like a lot more work,"

"Yes, there is going to be extra work here so we will train Maria to handle the bulk of the preparation while you concentrate on meeting with the clients. You're going to do a lot of delegating to Maria. She can handle it. That will keep you focused on the money-making tasks."

Scott starting shifting uneasily in his seat indicating he is growing uncomfortable. He said, "That sounds awfully complicated and a lot of work. I don't know if I can do it."

"You can do it, but not all at once. We are going to phase it in gradually. Remember our goals are retaining clients, making enough money to buy-out Robert. These new clients need to know that you are up to the task."

Most people cannot implement major changes and make it stick. Studies show that only one out of nine people can make major change in a short time. Eight out of nine cannot do it. Trying something new is viewed in the prefrontal cortex of the brain as a threat. Gradual adaptations, however are not viewed as a threat. Many people make change by gradually adapting to small, bite-size things. In order for someone to believe they can do it, they must first experience some level of success. That is what we will do for Scott and Maria. We will implement this in a measured, steady fashion and let them experience incremental success.

I said, "I'll keep my eye on the long view, while you focus on doing the first steps well. When the time is right we will introduce the next step, but only when Maria and you are ready. Is that alright?"

"I guess so. What's the cost of all this?" I told him the amount.

He said, "I'll have to run this by the Branch Manager because the company has to pay for this. Technically I am not allowed to pay for it myself."

"Okay, let me know as soon as you do. I can meet with him to explain the details if you want me to."

"I'll get back to you," he replied. I thought it would be fairly quick, but it was not.

Finally after a week Scott called. "We can only start to work on the stay in touch part and some system processes. My manager doesn't want me to start a new client service model or annual advisory fees. So the company will only pay for the first part. He says there is too much change."

"That is too bad. Okay, well we've got to start somewhere. Let's you and I meet on Tuesday."

By Tuesday, Maria rearranged appointments to free up a half-day for Scott and me. He and I will meet for the first two hours, then the three of us meet for two additional hours. That should be enough to lay out the plan of action steps for the first phase of the stay in touch program.

Our purpose is to design a program to communicate with all the clients with three goals. First, reassure them that their interests were being well cared for. Second, let them know how Robert is doing because many of them care a great deal for him since they have a decade-long relationship. Third, promote Scott as a knowledgeable advisor.

Our plan includes tactics to use with the category A, B, and C clients he had already defined. Category A clients include the 65 largest account groups. Category B is the 345 midsize account groups, while category C is the smallest account groups. We moved some B's up to A's and some C's to B's in recognition of referral champions, niche relationships, and family relationships.

A-level clients will be targeted for extra special attention with one-on-one meetings and phone calls. They will get multiple emails and letters in a sequence over a six-week period to warm, build, and nurture their relationship with Scott. We actually wrote rough drafts of each email and letter. We brainstormed the talking points for the phone calls. This was a short-term campaign for staying in touch. Designing a long-term campaign will come at a future meeting. For right now, first things first.

The next day, Wednesday, we met again for a half day to finalize the design for the client service system. We needed to formalize some type of format that Scott and Maria could prepare and execute repetitively. Robert had no standard format, but he had a certain style that worked for him. That was not going to work for Scott.

The system we worked on was not my preferred format. Company management was holding him to a basic format with two levels; premium and standard.

Premium level involved two meetings per year to review their accounts and talk about financial planning. He would try to get them to pay for a comprehensive financial analysis. This is for A-level clients and some B-level clients.

Standard level has one meeting per year to review accounts and discuss financial planning. This level is for B and C level clients.

For all meetings, Scott and Maria will produce a deliverable package with the agenda, observations, critical issues, and actionable recommendations. Together we drafted a standard template for the deliverable package and defined steps in a preparation process for them to follow.

Our plan is to monitor results of these meetings and make adjustments as needed. We agreed to teleconference weekly.

The excitement in Scott and Maria was evident when we finished the meeting. Scott was ready to get moving. There's a lot of opportunity in shaping the business in your own mold and make a lot of money. The *Wall of Frustration* in front of him was fading. The big problem was solved. He has a clear path to follow with the help of his teammate Maria.

11

PETER
PURSUING THE PRIZE

Two weeks after the meeting in Peter's home office, I called to continue the transition. He had made progress. The client list was organized into the A-B-C categorization. He found the Book of Business report that allowed him to identify the best clients and rank them. He identified products to reposition to provide recurring revenue, doing this with the help of the managing agent who was mindful of compliance issues. Peter had done what I asked of him, but that was it.

When asked if he had given any thoughts regarding the client service model and booking appointments, he was evasive. Said he was too busy to schedule a bunch of appointments in advance. Also he made no effort to arrange for an assistant.

He is still traveling to see clients, no meetings in his office, all meetings at their location. The drive time between appointments severely limits the number of clients he sees each week. Also he has not done anything regarding the new deliverable template idea. Not enough time, he says. He continues to do it the old way.

Consulting progress with him is going to be much slower than I hoped. How much effort is he willing to devote to change? Is his desire to achieve greater success sufficient enough to overcome his resistance to change? That is the limiting factor in whether or not he will make it to the next level. So I will have to motivate him to stretch and focus on the benefits of a little more change. Right now he views the multiple tasks of preparing for meetings as insurmountable obstacles. That is his current *Wall of Frustration*. It is going to take a team to break through it.

The number one practice in *The Business Breakout Blueprint®* is *build a team and delegate*. Peter needs an assistant to do all the preparation tasks that will allow him to focus on seeing clients.

A person can <u>add</u> to their income it they work harder and longer. Conversely, if they hire someone to assist, they can <u>multiply</u> their income. A qualified assistant can do all the systematic tasks that are important and necessary yet require little creativity. That frees the producer to do the critical tasks of producing income that only they can do. Working together as a team produces far greater results. That is the conversation I had with Peter.

"You are continuing to bang your head against the wall. You're limiting the number of clients you see and the amount of new business you write by driving to see clients. Also you're still doing everything yourself. There are only so many tasks you can do. You need help if you're ever going to break through. This is not the way to double your income. Let's find someone who can work for you part-time. Maybe an associate has an assistant who needs additional hours."

"Well. I'll think about it. Right now I've got to go across town to see a guy. We can talk again in two weeks at our regular time."

He is paying for my time and wisdom, but I am not going to keep doing this if he continues resisting necessary change. I will find someone else who is willing to go through change to succeed.

A week later and unexpected surprise occurs. He sends an email describing how he is implementing the client service model. The email reveals renewed energy as business seems to have picked up. He tells a story of a client implementing his recommendations with the new meeting format. He is still going out for the appointments, but is coming around to see the benefit of meeting in his office.

A week later on our scheduled conference call, he says, "Hey, I've decided to move into office space available within the agency. A space opened up when another agent left the business. The manager called me yesterday. He also said I can get support by sharing an assistant with another advisor. I'll use her to schedule appointments and prepare for meetings. There's a small conference meeting room I can use for appointments. Now I can get clients to come to me. And it is all affordable."

"That sounds great. Sounds like things are working out."

"Yes and there's more. A junior advisor seems interested in a joint arrangement. He will handle my C-level clients on a split-commission arrangement. That will free up a lot of my time to serve the A-clients. Of course we've got a lot of details to iron out. Now I'll be able to implement all those ideas you recommended. Thanks a bunch. Now let's figure out how to do it."

So this is working out after all. He is on the way to breaking through his *Wall of Frustration*. We have increased his production by implementing a new clients service model which lets him see clients regularly and close bigger sales. We are increasing recurring revenue and building stronger relationships which will boost the value of his practice when he decides to sell. In the end he is progressively achieving his goals.

12

CATHY
THE BREAKTHROUGH
BEGINS

Wednesday came when Cathy arrived precisely on-time at my home for a meeting in my front office. She greeted me through a bright smile. "I want to thank you for all the guidance. It has really helped me," she said as we settled into chairs.

"Well, that's good to hear. You are welcome. And, I am proud of you for taking action on the advice."

"Well, it's made a big difference for me. Things are going well. I've got business in the pipeline and five promising new appointments scheduled in the next few days. The stay-in-touch campaign is supplementing my other marketing activities. It is taking away a lot of stress."

"Oh, that is terrific, Cathy. But you had better be ready for what comes next. The pace of things are going to pick up with all the new business. Are you ready?"

"I think so. Joe, an associate, and I are thinking about hiring another person to help out. They will assist putting together our financial plan proposals and processing applications. They will work in tandem with Shirley who is doing the part-time marketing support."

"So you are growing and putting together a team. That's terrific. What will be the employment arrangement?"

"We are thinking of making it fulltime."

"What about payroll issues, income tax withholding, and workman's compensation? Which of you will handle that?"

"That's the thing we are kicking around."

"Well, who does it for Shirley?"

"I just pay her cash directly every week. She likes it that way. Besides it avoids going through the branch manager's payroll system where her hours will bump up from part-time to full time and she must be given benefits. The manager doesn't want to do that."

"Cathy, you can't pay the new person that way. You have to set up a structured system. There are two choices as I see it. One, you do it yourself, setup payroll, write checks, pay income tax withholding, pay workman's comp, provide benefits, and all the other required HR issues. If you are comfortable with all that then go ahead."

"Neither of us want to get into all that."

"Or, alternatively, let an employee leasing agency do it all. That's the way my partners and I did it. Worked out great. The agency helps you find and interview someone.

Once hired, the employee reports to you, does the tasks you assign, and works at your location. For all practical purposes, they are your employee. The important difference is that the employee's pay check comes from the leasing agency. The benefits package is provided by the agency. The agency performs all the payroll and HR duties. All you have to do is pay the agency."

"How much?"

"As a broad estimate, the total cost to you is the salary plus 25% to 30%. That covers the cost of benefits, employer Social Security matching, workman's comp, and the agency fee. It is worth it. It takes away many of the headaches of managing employees and lets you focus on growing the business. That was one of the best decisions my partners and I made."

"This is really useful information. I'll talk to Joe about it."

"Good. Let's get back to the new planning clients. What kind of service plan are you bringing them in on?"

"What do you mean?"

"Sounds like they are coming in as financial planning clients where they pay a fee, but what are their expectations for future service and fees?"

"Well, after we get all the initial implementation, we will meet with them whenever we need to review accounts."

"Do you pre-schedule these meetings? I mean, at the end of one meeting, do you schedule the next one for three to six months in advance?"

"No," she said.

"Cathy, I am delighted that things are going well right now. Yet, I can see another wall of frustration rising up six to nine months from now. You're going to be faced with scheduling follow-up review meetings with these clients while still prospecting for new business. That problem is going to sink into an endless rut."

"Well, what do I do?"

"Have I ever told you about Type-V service? It will eliminate that wall of frustration before it even rises. Plus it will set you up for future recurring income."

"No, what is it?"

"Imagine clients looking forward to meeting with you every four months to get new, useful information about their financial goals. Imagine them implementing those new ideas with new products when it makes sense. And imagine them paying you a fee every year to be part of this service. Does that sound like a system you would like to offer?"

"Yes, sure."

"Now that is a Type-V service. The 'V' stands for value. You deliver additional value at each of the three annual meetings. Each of these meetings are preplanned. The client always knows what is coming next. And since you pre-schedule them, that eliminates a lot of hours calling around trying to schedule new service appointments. Plus your production grows tremendously. It's a win-win. The clients get ongoing, value-added service, while you get higher production and less frustration. Sound good?"

"Heck yes."

"All right. It's time for us to move into a consulting relationship where I will show you exactly how to do all this and you pay me a fee that's affordable."

Cathy is on her way to really breaking through to the next level. So far she has improved marketing effectiveness with the stay in touch system. She is building a team to leverage strengths and be more productive. She will build a unique client service system that will differentiate her from the competition and produce greater revenue.

13

SCOTT
TAKING CONTROL

I remember a time filled with anticipation as I began a journey to a destination promising fun and excitement. That was the emotion Scott and Maria shared, excited to implement the strategies developed at the last meeting and excited to have a clear plan to break through the *Wall of Frustration*. They implemented the stay-in-touch system and client service model.

Weeks passed as many clients responded positively. They accepted with regret the knowledge that Robert is out of their lives. Some reached out with cards and letters while a couple of them actually visited Robert, but walked away sad as they witnessed the severity of his speech disability. Robert was happy he had not been forgotten.

The new format for client service meetings also seems to work well. Scott and Maria are scheduling up to twenty appointments per week, packed tightly one after another in the office. They are able to efficiently prepare, conduct, and follow-up on the meetings. Scott is closing on new business as well. These new, full commissions help augment the reduced payout from the split-commissions. He is extremely busy with little time to talk with me on the phone for the weekly monitoring sessions, so instead I talk with Maria.

Over the weeks a few clients with average size accounts transfer to various other financial institutions, not surprisingly since they probably had pre-existing relationships with the other brokers even while working with Robert. They just wanted to consolidate with someone they know.

It is four months later when I get the call from Scott. Something is up because it is Thursday not Friday at our regular time and he is calling me instead of the other way around. "This has been a bad week. Maria just got a call from another broker's office. The Jensens are moving their account. They are one of my biggest accounts. And that is the second one this week. The Hadlers moved their account earlier this week. And you recall that another one left two weeks ago. What's happening?"

"I'm not sure. Did you get any indication of dissatisfaction?"

"No, yes, well not really. The Jensens were scheduled to come in for a follow-up meeting next week, but called to cancel. Today, the other broker's office called."

"Well I suggest you call the Jensens to see if they will tell you why. They may or may not take your call. Tell them you are sorry to see them go. You want them to stay, but if they are determined to leave, please tell you why. What are they missing here?"

"I'll call them later this afternoon. I've got three back-to-back appointments starting in ten minutes. Let's skip tomorrow's call and talk next week."

"Sure, let me know how things go with the Jensens."

Early afternoon the next day I get an email from Scott. Desperation and frustration apparent in the short note. "I need help quickly. Can we meet for a late breakfast tomorrow. I know it is Saturday, but I've got to talk."

The Village Inn could be a twin for IHOP except for color scheme. It is clean, well decorated in springtime colors, and busy. They are always busy. On weekdays business people meet to talk business. On weekends it is mostly family.

Both Scott and I arrive five minutes early and have to wait seven minutes for a booth. We ordered. The coffee comes quickly, we take sips and he starts talking.

"The message from the Jensens was tough to hear. They are not mad at me, I did nothing wrong. It is just that they want more. More of what they couldn't say. Then it struck me, I saw it coming, but didn't recognize it. Not just from them, but from others as well." He wraps both hands around the warm coffee cup as if it gives him strength. "And now I clearly see that I may lose a couple more big clients if I don't do something different. I've got to step up my game quickly, but I don't know what to do."

We stopped talking as the server brought the meals. Scott added salt and pepper to his eggs automatically before tasting it.

My mind wandered to a story of Admiral Hyman Rickover's view of this. He was the father of the U.S. Navy's nuclear power propulsion program and a legend for his intensity and focus. He interviewed every officer coming into the nuclear power program. I was one of the candidates to endure one of his highly unorthodox interviews.

There is one story where he asked the candidate, "Do you salt and pepper your food before you taste it?" When the officer said yes the Admiral threw him out. Admiral Rickover did not want officers in the program who took action before understanding the facts of the situation.

But, that was not my story. As an officer candidate within several months of being commissioned a Navy Ensign, I sat in front of him for two or three minutes as he asked rapid-fire questions. I struggled to answer before the next question. I did not want to go into the nuclear power program, instead I wanted to go to naval flight school and told him so. Not pleased he yelled, "Get the hell out of my office, I don't ever want to see you again." My flight response kicked in and I was moving towards the door midway through his tirade. The fiercest butt-chewing I ever received.

Scott said, "What are you smiling about?"

"Oh, nothing. Just a story about salting and peppering food. I'll tell you about it over a glass of beer sometime.

Let's get back on topic. Do you think you are giving good financial advice? I mean have the clients shown dissatisfaction with the quality of your advice?"

"No, not at all. It's just routine stuff, asset allocation, rebalancing and the like. I offer financial planning if they seem open to it. There's nothing wrong with the advice."

"Well then, it sounds like it has a lot to do with perception. Consider this, is it the value they perceive or the value they actually get? You may be victim of underestimating the importance of perceived value. I'll tell you what I mean and how we can fix it."

As we ate our breakfast I described the notion of reframing how people view a product. I repeat a story told by Rory Sutherland at a TED Talk in 2009. It is the story of the potato and how it went from being viewed as just a disgusting root to a royal, desired vegetable.

In the fifteenth century, Spanish sailors brought potatoes back to Europe when they returned from South America with silver. But in Europe many people refused to grow or eat potatoes. In the eighteenth century Frederick the Great of Prussia wanted the Germans to adopt the potato, grow it and eat it. He wanted to lower the risk of famine. He realized that two crops to fall back on, wheat and potatoes, is better that just one when a bad growing season occurs. The only problem was the Prussians ate very few vegetables. So he tried making it compulsory to grow potatoes, but that did not work out. The Prussian peasantry refused. So he tried a marketing solution.

He declared the potato a Royal vegetable and none but the Royal family could grow it or eat it. He planted it in a Royal potato patch with guards who had instructions to guard over it, but not to guard it very well. Now it is human nature that if something is worth guarding it is worth stealing. Before long there was a massive underground potato growing operation in Germany. What he effectively did was rebrand the potato and elevate its perceived value by reframing how people looked at it. It was the same potato, but now valued and desired.

"So what does that story mean for you? We are going to elevate the perceived value of your client experience by making a few adjustments, change the name to the *Comprehensive Assessment Program*, and raise the fee."

Over the next forty minutes we talked and ate. The plates were cleared and we continued talking as the server brought a fresh carafe of coffee. I told him that we would be a while, but not to worry. I will take care of him with the tip to offset the loss of the table to other customers.

I proceeded to describe the *Comprehensive Assessment Program* as a new premium level of service targeting clients desiring higher value service. The program will be rolled out carefully to them. Some other clients who may not recognize or appreciate added value will continue getting the previous level of service. For both levels of service we committed to verifying the quality of delivery.

The *Comprehensive Assessment Program* consists of three meetings per year each focused on different themes. Taken together, they deliver comprehensive financial advice that meets fiduciary standards. Clients will pay an annual fee to be a part of it.

- *The Personal Economic Assessment* updates key accumulation goals including retirement, college funding, and financial position plus reviews investment accounts.

- *The Life Focus Assessment* reviews estate planning and insurance protection plus reviews investment accounts.

- *The Tax Status Assessment* reviews issues affecting their taxes this year plus reviews investment accounts.

I suggest that he offer this to all clients. Some will accept it and some will not. The ones who will not accept it will stay in their current service level. The ones accepting it will be High Value Clients who appreciate greater value and willingly pay more to get it. Surprisingly a high percentage of A-level clients and some B-level will probably do it. Why will a high percentage accept it? I suspect that clients in an advisory relationship are already predisposed to want high value advice.

Next I described how to make his meeting presentations new and unique. He is going to position these meetings similar to a boardroom executive briefing and we will call it the *Boardroom Presentation System*.

I said, "If clients are looking for something new and different, this is it. You are going to need a 36 inch, flat-panel TV to mount on the wall that is Bluetooth capable to communicate with your computer. They are very affordable now. I can help install it, it is no big deal."

Over the next cup of coffee I described how the *Boardroom Presentation System* works. Clients and advisor sit around his conference table facing the wall-mounted TV viewing a PowerPoint presentation sent via Bluetooth from his computer. The PowerPoint slide deck is a template for the appropriate Assessment theme. It is customized with the client's information. Its agenda covers observations of their current situation, identifies critical issues, and presents specific, actionable recommendations. While viewing and discussing, clients can take notes on the printed handout given to them. It is the package of PowerPoint slides bound with a cover.

"They will be impressed, believe me. I did this while in active practice and the clients loved it. The meeting conversation stays on point projecting authority. Clients accept most recommendations with less push back. You will look different from other advisors in their eyes because nobody else does it this way. As an added benefit, . you and Maria can prepare efficiently for each meeting because it's built upon a template system. I'll show you how." He was excited

Scott is a determined person. During the following week, he persisted in selling the idea to his manager. The manager objected, but Scott kept at it even saying that failure would be partly the manager's fault for standing in his way. He is not going to let this business opportunity slip away from him. He is determined to succeed. The manager decides it is best to let Scott move ahead or he will never hear the end of it..

Looking back, Scott ran into one *Wall of Frustration*, broke through it, grew upward, ran into another wall, broke through that one and continued growing. If he runs into another one that slows his momentum, he can look to the practices in *The Business Breakout Blueprint*® to find a solution to solve it? I am confident he will find a way to break through that future wall as well.

PART IV

The Business Breakout Blueprint®

Practice 1

BUILD A TEAM AND DELEGATE

Mother's remedies to cure family illnesses are passed down from generation to generation because they work. They are not the only cure for the problem, but they work. So it is for best practices to run a business. There are many prudent models that deliver results. Here are five business practices proven as solid footers in the foundation of a successful small business.

In the early days of running a business entrepreneurs want to do everything themselves because they have the time, but not the money. As the business grows, they continue doing the mechanics of operating the business plus handling all the random problems that pop up. They grow aggravated as they are unable to spend time thinking how to grow the business. This is the *Wall of Frustration*. Ironically success and increased volume have created this natural barrier. Too many small business owners accept this predicament and live with it. Achievers, however look for ways to overcome obstacles. The first actions to deal with the obstacles are building a team and delegating. Then incorporate systematic processes to make things more efficient..

Build a Team

You can <u>add</u> to your income by working harder or getting another job. On the other hand, you can <u>multiply</u> your income by hiring someone to help you do more. Building a team is the first significant step in dealing with work overload.

A business owner is best suited for guiding the direction of the business and looking for growth opportunities. It is a waste of entrepreneurial resources to spend valuable time doing the mechanics of the business when it can be done at lower cost by an employee. This is true if and only if you, the owner, use the time to greater purpose. Identify the things only you can do or must do. Then delegate the other tasks to someone else.

I have come across it numerous times when talking with small business owners. When I mention that I am writing a book entitled "Stop Banging Your Head," they frequently say, "That's a great title. I feel like I am always banging my head. I've got to stop it." After some probing, it is revealed they are typically overwhelmed with doing production tasks in the business. The obvious solution is delegating some tasks to an employee who may be on staff already.

An assistant, with proper delegation, can do the things that have to be done, but not by you. This frees you to continue doing the critical things that can only be done by you to make money and grow.

When To Hire

The signal to hire someone is when you have a backlog of tasks to perform to get to closing. There is money on the shelf ready to be made, but you are slow getting to it. That is the signal to hire someone.

Another signal may be when you are the rainmaker, but are getting bogged down processing a case for the previous client. You are unable to go out and bring in new business. It is time to transfer processing tasks to someone else.

The signals are clear. It is just a matter of doing it.

What Tasks To Delegate

Entrepreneurs frequently find it difficult to delegate. It seems easier to do it themselves than to take time to train someone else. That may be true for a one-off task, but not for repetitive tasks. The business owner must get out from under those tasks. Here are steps to identify things that should be delegated.

1. Identify all the tasks that need to be performed.
2. Tag each one as Critical, Important, or Routine.
3. Tag those that only you can do because of licensing, etc.

4. Tag each one regarding whether you <u>like</u> to do it, or you <u>don't like</u> to do it.
5. Identify those items that a) only you can do, b) are critical/important things, <u>and</u> c) you like to do. These are your tasks.
6. Delegate all other tasks.

Manage To Expectations

Set clear expectations for employees. Tell them what you expect of them. Be clear and remain consistent. Set high expectations and manage to their fulfillment. When someone meets and exceeds the expectation then take the time to praise them. When someone fails to meet expectation then address it right away, in private.

Form, Storm, Norm, Then Perform

As you build your team, expect to encounter some bumps in the road. Whether you are hiring your first team member or hiring your fifth, the team members (including you) generally go through four natural stages as their relationships develop. The process could take a few days or up to several months. Try not to get upset. Just put on your calm manager hat and work through it.

Form. As you bring people together they are initially polite and try to understand their roles. Some hold back their real personalities while they get to know the others.

Storm. Soon thereafter, people get into their jobs and may start to argue about tasks or about personal idiosyncrasies that were left unsaid in the early stage. As the leader, you must step in and resolve differences that might otherwise cause continuing aggravation and performance disruption. Do it diplomatically yet firmly.

Norm. After the conflicts and minor irritations are sorted out, team members begin to cooperate and help out one another. Their focus turns toward the tasks to perform and getting them done efficiently.

Perform. As the team relationships mature, you will see them working more smoothly as a team. Under your guidance productivity increases. Encourage them to find additional ways to improve processes

All teams go through this process. Expect it and deal with it. Then you will witness the Wall of Frustration crumbling as more projects are completed in shorter amounts of time. Your profits grow along with your level of satisfaction.

Some People Are Not A Good Fit

Square pegs do not fit into rounds holes. Some tasks are not good fits for some people. When that occurs, deal with it directly. It may be a simple matter of shifting their roles to other tasks that are a better fit. Then again, it may be their internal value system is incompatible with your organization. That does not mean they are bad people. On the contrary, they may be good people in the wrong role. When that occurs, let them go. It is not worth it to keep them on. Bad fits develop into their own Wall of Frustration. Plus it is not fair to the employee to keep them in the wrong role. Fix it as soon as you realize it is happening.

Compensate With A Purpose

Determining how much to pay them and how to motivate them is always tricky. Compensating employees is about more than just money and benefits. It is paying them enough so they are satisfied plus providing other things that motivate them to exceed. Consider these two methods.

Money, Marbles and Chalk method. *Money* is the level of compensation they can be proud of plus bonuses for great work. *Marbles* are awards that recognize their achievement. And *Chalk* is written recognition and public acknowledgement recognizing their achievements. It works well for clearly defined tasks where only a low level of creativity is needed.

Money, Autonomy, Mastery and Purpose method. *Money* is a compensation level they can reasonably expect to achieve. *Autonomy* addresses their urge to direct their own lives with flexibility in work hours and methods. *Mastery* fulfills the desire to get better at something that matters like being the best at what they do. *Purpose* fulfills the yearning to do what they do in service of something larger than themselves, such as a noble mission. It is a compensation framework best suited where creativity and results-oriented efforts are needed.

Rewards and bonuses narrow the focus and channel the mind. They are good for structured tasks and mechanical skills. Rewards do not work so well for creative solutions. The downside to bonuses is they may lose their attraction as an extra benefit. When bonuses are given regularly there becomes an expectation that they are part of the compensation package. Be careful how you implement them. Tie the level of bonus directly to results of tasks completely under their control. Organization-wide bonuses easily become expected regularly and lose their incentive value.

Outsourcing

Hiring and managing employees brings with it a new level of complication that add to the complexity of running a business. You can do it yourself or out-source it. I highly recommend out-sourcing using a staffing agency rather than trying to save money and do all the human resources tasks yourself.

Years ago when my partnership group moved out of the corporation's regional office we were faced with the a critical issue. How were we going to manage the staff? Previously our staff were employees of the parent corporation. All human resources issues were handled by the company. Once we moved out they became our direct employees where we manage payroll, benefits and other human resources issues. We asked ourselves whether we should do it ourselves or use the services of a staffing agency? We chose the staffing agency. That turned out to be a wise decision.

The agency became our virtual human resources department handling payroll, benefit programs, human resource compliance issues and more. All we had to do was write a check for compensation, benefits, and surcharge. The agency did all the other work.

Our staff looked and acted like direct employees of us, we directly supervised them. However, the staff pay checks showed the logo of the leasing agency. The staff was happy and we were happy.

Consider outsourcing for other areas as well. Consider expanding your thinking beyond immediate support staff. Consider outsourcing for digital/social media marketing and new associate training. Build a virtual team of professionals that free you to do what you are good at rather than get bogged down in areas you are not good at. Think "outside the box."

Systematize Production Processes

Want efficiency in your business? If something has to be done over and over again, consider establishing a step by step process to get it done. This works with one-person projects as well as multi-person projects such as preparing for client meetings. It is a key way to break through the frustration barrier. Automate and systematize processes that are repetitive and do not require new creativity. Existing tasks become easier and more gets done in less time. Now you have the time to take on new projects.

Power of Repeatable Processes

Automating and systemizing processes is more than making you efficient. It is also reassuring to clients when they get predictably good service. When you add new team members that interact with clients, the processes will be of comfort to clients. Ultimately when you sell your practice and move on, the predictable processes will reassure clients and generate greater loyalty and low turnover.

Automation begins by developing standard operating procedures that can be followed with machine-like consistency. Record them in a procedures manual to follow again and again.

Start out simply. Use a three ring binder and label it *YourCompany Operations Manual.* Hand-write procedures as you encounter them. Later on you can type them. After that, add tabs to divide procedures according to subject matter. Your manual will grow and grow and continue to be more useful.

Better still, have your staff create the manual under your guidance. As they perform tasks, tell them to write down the steps. Stick to it. Use it to train new staff as you grow or when a new hire replaces a departed employee.

An excellent best-selling book, *The E-Myth Revisited* written by Michael E. Gerber describes the power of this. My high recommendation of it is an understatement. It is a must-read for small business owners.

In your operating manual, formulate processes for:
- Following up with prospects
- Integrating new clients
- Servicing existing clients

Build these procedures gradually as you need them. Do not try to build them all at once. That will surely lead to stagnation.

Follow-up Campaigns

Build follow-up procedures for commonly faced situations; call them campaigns. Within each campaign, create follow-up sequences to deal with specific situations. For example, you may have a Prospect Campaign, a Sales Offer Campaign, etc.

The Prospect Campaign may have several specific follow-up sequences for referrals, seminars, signup on a website form, and direct-mail response. The follow-up steps will be built around phone scripts and email templates.

Here is an example. Consider this sequence to follow-up after a seminar.

Day-1: Contact person at their preferred contact method (phone, email). Schedule appointment. If unable to reach them, place into the short-term sequence.

Day-2: Send email saying unable to reach you, I'll try again. summarize key messages from the seminar. Call again.

Day-4: Send email, summarize benefits others are getting. Ask to meet.

Day-6: Send email, ... call again.

Day-8: Send email sorry we are unable to connect. I will stay in touch with periodic messages that may be useful to you. Place into long-term follow-up sequence.

Create similar sequences to follow-up with referrals and other prospects. Follow-up with everyone the same way so no one falls through the crack and you know what to do next with each one.

Systematize Client Service Processes

Make the processes for preparing for routine interactions an efficient assembly line procedure. This may range from new Client Engagement, to preparation for client service meetings, and to implementing actions following meetings. All are prepared the same way.

Define steps for what needs to be done, how to do it, and who is responsible for doing it. Establish timelines for getting each step done.

Automate Marketing Systems

Over eighty percent of prospects look you up online before meeting with you. That is why you better have a professional looking presence including a company website, LinkedIn profile, and Facebook business fan page. Begin with some simple things online.

Your company's website should be professional looking including critical elements, such as contact information, what you do, how you do it, who you do it for, how to get started, and a web entry form to fill-out to get more information. The web entry form is an essential step in building your contact list.

Build a LinkedIn profile and make posts periodically. Always include a relevant image to go along with the text message. Images are easily found by entering a keyword in Google and looking at images associated with that word.

Create a Facebook business fan page and make posts weekly as a minimum. Always include a relevant image or video. Get in the habit of sharing resources posted by others.

Five Habits Of Effective Leaders

As the owner of your own small business you are clearly the upfront leader of the team. Do you find that a comfortable role? Some people are natural leaders, but most are not. I fell into the latter category and thus was compelled to figure out what to do. Over time I compiled this list of five habits to define what I needed to do as a leader.

1. Continually communicate a strategic vision. Tell my team members about the company mission. Remind them of our core values. Do it regularly. Let them learn to stay focused. Remember, people

don't know what you think, they only know what you say and what you do.

2. <u>Tell others what you expect of them.</u> Do it as soon as they join the team. Be clear and hold them to it.

3. <u>Focus on key tasks.</u> Let team members be constantly aware that you are most focused on things that matter most. That does not imply you ignore small things, deal with them as necessary. Remember, *people focus on what you focus on.*

4. <u>Be consistent.</u> Do these first three things consistently. Let team members understand that you are driving in one direction. Avoid frequent changes of priorities.

5. <u>Communicate success enthusiastically.</u> Celebrate small and big successes. Do it loudly. Team members like to be part of successful projects and successful organizations. Brag about it.

You may also apply these habits of leadership in other roles including membership on boards of directors in community organizations or charities, social groups, and others.

<u>Summary</u>

Breakthrough your *Wall of Frustration* by forming a team. Employees, whether part-time or full-time, take routine jobs that the rainmaker – you – should not be doing. Let them empower you to think, plan, and grow the business. Empower them to be more efficient by establishing systematic processes for getting routine projects accomplished. Your income will grow rapidly when you get the team working together to increase capacity.

Practice 2

DIFFERENTIATE YOURSELF WITH PREMIUM DELIVERY

It is not enough to be the best at what you do, rather it is being the only one who delivers it the way you do.

Bill Van Hoy

Many other professionals in your type of business deliver the same services as you. Some are capable of delivering high quality equal to yours. So, how do you stand out? Most advice suggests that you strive to become more an expert in your field. That is good advice. But, when you are already at expert level, how much better can you get? Not much. As a matter of fact, this is the hardest way to differentiate yourself. Then how do you differentiate yourself to standout in the eyes of your perfect clients?

For me it began with understanding two intersecting concepts. First, people don't buy things, they buy solutions to problems. They buy things that solve their big underlying problems. The second understanding is that it may not be enough to deliver expert solutions, rather it is delivering the solutions with unique, premium delivery.

Solving the underlying problem, is why I became a financial planner. In financial services, one of the big problems of clients is worrying they don't have control of where they are going and how to use their resources to get there. That's what I wanted for myself years ago.

It began while I was on active-duty in the US Navy. My wife and I wanted an advisor to help put our financial matters into perspective. We had a respectable stock brokerage account, good income and other resources. Our big-firm stockbroker was always trying to sell us the next best stock. Our insurance agent was trying to sell us more insurance coverage. There was nothing wrong with either of those. It is just that we wanted someone to help focus it all. That was our big underlying issue.

We attended a three-part financial planning seminar program which was well done. I got a lot out of it and was excited to meet one-on-one with the planner at the third session. The advisor prepared a financial analysis based upon the data we provided at the second seminar session. I had high hopes.

The advisor went through the analysis which was informative. Then he made one recommendation, apply for a universal life insurance policy. He did not address investments or retirement planning or how to pull it all together which was our big underlying issue. I was disappointed.

While insurance was a legitimate issue, it did not address my primary reason for meeting with him. I wanted advice and how to manage what we had already accumulated and how to invest for the future. He failed to address that. So we did no business with him.

Frustrated with that advisory approach I told myself, I could do that. I decided to become a financial advisor once I completed Navy service. I was determined to help people get their arms around all their financial issues in a comprehensive way. I was going to listen, then deliver.

In the year before my retirement date, I enrolled in the Certified Financial Planner (CFP®) program at the College for Financial Planning. One year later after transitioning, I joined a national financial planning firm. My CFP training coupled with company training got me off to a fast start. I brought with me a vision of how I wanted to deal with my new clients. I told them I wanted to help them get their arms around all their financial issues. That resonated with many of them.

I began creating a system that summarized and tracked progress towards financial goals based upon how I would want it presented to me. It evolved into a unique approach to present financial advice to clients. That is how I got started differentiating myself.

You see, it is not good enough to be the best at what you do, rather it is being the only one that does it the way you do. That is how you differentiate. Deliver your service in a memorable way that addresses the core concerns of your clients.

Perceived Value

Often being different involves a good bit of perception – how you are perceived. Perceived value is sometimes just as important as real value. Perceived value is the worth of a service in the mind of the client. Their perception of the value of the service affects the price they're willing to pay. It changes the way they look at things.

The power of reframing the way people look at things is extremely important. The greater the perceived value, the more likely a person will select the service and pay a premium price. Too often, professionals providing a personal service get preoccupied with providing the service the same way others do, just done with greater care and accuracy. That is not wrong, it is not enough. They lose sight that a small change in the way people look at it makes a big difference in how they enjoy it. Impressions have a fantastic effect on what people do.

For example, consider two cups of coffee, one from 7-11 and the other from Starbucks. A small 12 ounce coffee at 7-11 costs $1.25. A Tall coffee at Starbucks (also 12 oz.) costs $1.70. That is 40% more than 7-11. Both are good coffees, but Starbucks gets more because of their environment – community seating, spa music, chatty service.

Now consider a Tall Vanilla Latte at Starbucks, it costs $3.40. They take the same 12 ounce cup of coffee, add some frothy milk, add a little flavoring, give it a fancy name, then double the price. <u>Double</u> the price! It is the perception of added value that supports the price.

At 7-11, you walk over to the coffee station, pour your own coffee, add cream and sugar, go to the counter, and pay the courteous attendant. There is no attempt at adding perceived value.

Walk into a Starbucks you see people sitting around reading books working on their computers or chatting with one another. You walk up to the counter and the attendant carries on polite conversation with you while you look at all the menu options. There are muffins, sandwiches, and of course coffee. You get to select the size, Tall, Grande, or Venti. So many choices. All this time there is a spa background music playing overhead.

Both places have good coffee – I actually like 7-11 coffee better – but I'm willing to pay more at Starbucks because of the overall experience.

Then there is the tip cup beside the cash register at Starbucks. Most people toss in something. You don't see a tip cup at 7-11. Why can Starbucks do that? It is the perceived value. People get more enjoyment from things of greater perceived value and are willing to pay more to get premium services with higher perceived value. It absolutely works – perceived value adds to profits.

Differentiate Yourself With Premium Services

Chances are, if you are reading this book, you are providing some kind of a service solution that solves problems for people. How do you turn a standard service into a premium service? It is more than just making it bigger.

Start with a standard service. Then add features, benefits, enhanced packaging, and more personalized engagement. Give it a new name too. Now you have a premium service. It is half additional real value and half perceived value.

Naming Your Services and Processes

Your premium offering should look and sound unique.

"Nothing is a big deal unless you big-deal-it yourself." That is what Terry Conti, my former professional coach taught me. And big-dealing it begins with impactful names. Starbucks does it is with cup sizes. They do not call them small, medium, and large. Instead they are Tall, Grande, and Venti.

Another example, consider how you name your engagement meetings. Do you call them account review meetings or "Comprehensive Assessments?" Which sounds more substantial? They may involve the same content, but the name delivers weight. A client may be willing to pay a fee for involvement in a "Comprehensive Assessment", but not just for a review meeting.

Enhanced packaging begins with naming. Words make a difference. Name your services, name your processes, and name your features. Proper selection of the name affects the value clients attach to it. It affects how much the clients are willing to pay. Do not be afraid to be outrageous, it will not sound that way to clients.

How do you name your unique process? Compose a name with the following three parts:

"The" + [Benefit Word/Phrase] + [Technology Word]

Here are representative Benefit Words:

Comprehensive	Discovery	Critical
Breakthrough	Personal	Vision

Here are representative Technology Words:

Process	Program	Assessment
Experience	Technology	Solution
Approach	Network	Technique
Method	System	Toolkit

Putting it all together, consider this example of an on-going service model for financial planning. Let's call it "The Financial Focus System." It consists of four engagements:

- The Personal Vision Focus – initial meeting

- The Discovery Interview – data gathering meeting
- The Critical Issues Briefing – presentation of observations
- The Breakthrough Solutions Experience – implement recommendations

These names convey to clients the importance you place upon each step. You want them to take it seriously and justify the fee they are paying. It is essential in solidifying the perceived value.

Consider Subscription Services

Add services constructed of periodic re-engagements. These are periodic meetings with clients for a specific purpose. Deliver it differently, keeping in mind the focus on solutions to problems. Charge a fee for the service.

Some businesses are based on recurring relationships like CPAs, dentists, lawn care, fitness centers, as examples. Other businesses are not routinely doing it, but they should. For example financial planners, photographers, estate attorneys, and insurance agents are not setting up recurring programs. They all should seriously figure out how to do it.

High Value Clients

Consider a premium pricing structure for delivering premium-level, added-value service. You will be surprised at how many people are attracted to the premium level based upon the extra real value. I call them High Value Clients.

High Value Clients are drawn to premium products with extra value even if it has a higher price. They appreciate greater value and pay more to get it when they can afford it. And they do not have to be rich. They are found in all economic levels.

I stumbled upon this revelation by accident. It was during the introduction of my new premium financial advisory service program which represented a change in the way clients received service. The previous conventional model involved account review meetings with clients once or twice a year at no additional charge

The objective of my new program was focusing on clients who truly valued my service. Simultaneously, I wanted to increase revenue from financial advice fees. I designed a new program delivering more benefits in a unique way.

My radical restructure would serve only clients that paid an annual fee for on-going comprehensive financial advice (Advisory Fee). These were not fees for managing money, they were separate. Clients choosing not to pay the annual advisory fee would be transferred to an associate advisor who did not charge the fee nor deliver the same benefits. It was a complete restructuring of my business model.

But here was the dilemma. What if a lot of them refused? What would I do then? I was actually scared to present it.

I chose to present it to clients this way. I said "I am restructuring my practice to focus more attention on clients who want comprehensive management of all their financial issues and want it on an ongoing basis. This is what the new program looks like."

Then I described the program of four Assessment engagements each year. I called it "Boardroom Level Service." It involved a fee to be paid each year instead of the fee they paid every three or four years for an update of the financial analysis. That was a big jump.

I told them, "I want you to be a part of this program. I believe it is a good fit for you, yet I realize it is a business decision for you. If you feel the regular Assessments are of great benefit, then come on over and join me. However, if you may feel there is not enough value for you compared to the previous program structure just tell me and I will let you work with my experienced associate who does not charge the annual fee. She will provide service the way you received it previously. You won't hurt my feelings because I realize it is just a business decision on your part." Then I mentally swallowed hard.

To my great surprise and delight, 80% of my clients agreed to upgrade to the premium service program. That was huge. It demonstrated the mindset of High Value Clients. They appreciate greater value and willingly pay more money to get it.

Boardroom Level Service

Typically at a review meeting, an advisor sits with clients around a table and shows them copies of account statements and other brochures. During the meeting the advisor slides statements back and forth across the table, highlights some areas on them, generally using them as the focal point of the conversation.

My "Boardroom Level Service" was different. I treated it like an executive briefing. We sat around a conference table facing a flat-panel display mounted on the wall. On it was displayed a briefing package of their financial status, critical issues, and recommendations. I call this a "boardroom experience." In fact, I introduced it to clients by saying, "If you're going down to Wall Street to be briefed by the largest investment banking firm and you know that you are their most important client, how do you expect to be treated? Pretty well, right? Well to the extent we can, you're going to be treated that way here."

I was "big dealing it."

That set the tone. I wanted to reframe how they felt about the meeting. In essence, it was a boardroom briefing. They regarded the recommendations more seriously and implemented most of them. They took notes on the briefing package we prepared for them. Note that there was no shuffling of account statements back and forth across the table.

As a unique kicker, while they were meeting with me I had a mobile auto detailer washing their car in the parking lot. The clients loved it! They were treated special. No other advisor in town did it that way. It showed I was different and unique.

I recall a time when some clients were sad when it was raining the day of their appointment and thought they would not get their car washed. I told them not to worry, I will send the detailer out to their house on a sunny day. Problem solved.

This is a premium service built upon a conventional model with enhanced packaging and more personalized engagement. People willing pay more for it and willing pay on a recurring basis. More about that later.

While this example is for a financial advisory practice, it can also be adopted by estate attorneys, tax accountants, portrait photographers, and others. For example, suppose an estate attorney also offers a "Family Estate Assurance Program." After drafting the will or trust, they meet annually to review family changes, tax law changes, and verify if old documents are still adequate. Also they could conduct small-group workshops for program members to educate them on estate and eldercare issues. For this program they charge an annual fee.

Photographers for example, can offer a "Life's Precious Moments Program" where they schedule photo shoots on selected annual events, such as birthdays, wedding anniversaries, holidays, graduations, or other special events. The photo sessions are covered by the annual program fee, but canvas photos and albums are extra.

The possibilities are endless for all sorts of businesses. Any business owner can do it. Solve a problem and do it with unique premium delivery.

Practice 3

STAY IN TOUCH WITH PROSPECTS AND CLIENTS

Finding prospects interested in doing business is the constant struggle faced by all small business entrepreneurs. Over the years, they meet dozens or even hundreds of people. Yet many of them don't want to do business right away. So the business owners have to devote additional effort, time and money attracting new prospects. But what happens to those people they already met? What happens to the ones that did not do business right away?

Some of those may want to do business in the future. Who will they do business with? The answer – they will do business with someone they know, they like, and they trust. That someone will be you if you stay in touch and become a trusted resource.

Years ago, my partners and I implemented a marketing plan to attract new clients with seminars. We started hosting workshops in libraries, then moved to buffet-style restaurants, then hotel banquet halls, and finally moved up to high-end restaurants. I spoke before groups as small as seven people and audiences as large as two hundred fifty people. I found that 25 to 30 people was the best size for interaction, intimacy and productivity.

Eventually, I got pretty good at closing the program and motivating people to request on the comment card to meet for a private consultation. Generally two-thirds to three-fourths did so.

In the weeks following, we met with half of those that signed up because some people changed their mind and others could not be reached. Two thirds of those we met were converted to clients. The other third were either unqualified or didn't see the value of our offering. That means 65% of those who showed interest at the seminar by giving their contact information, did not become clients right away? Yet they had some interest. Eventually, some will change their mind and want to do business. What happened to them? We got so busy integrating the new clients and servicing existing clients that we lost touch with them.

When we needed more new clients, we spent more money hosting another dinner-seminar. But what about the 65% from previous seminars? We lost contact. What a shame! In retrospect it was clear this was a lost opportunity. We spent all that money purchasing mailing lists, sending out high quality invitations, picking good venues, providing delicious meals, and valuable staff time.

Then we spent more money doing it all over again to attract more prospects. We failed to adequately stay in touch with ones we had already met.

A Three-Step System

Here's how to stay in touch with prospects you have previously met.

Step 1. Build a contact list of names, phone numbers and email addresses. That list is a gold mine. It's been done in a variety of ways from using contact relationship management programs, email service provider programs, Excel spreadsheets, and others. Clearly some are more useful than others. Pick an application that easily facilitates sending emails and other communications.

What's in a contact list? The very basic fields are name (first and last), email address, and phone number. Depending on the robustness of your application you will add fields for mailing address, salutation, job title, company name, etc.

Email address is the most crucial since emails are generally the easiest and most versatile way to stay in touch. I make it a practice to ask for an email address every time I ask for a phone number.

Step 2. Execute short-term follow-up campaigns targeting new prospects to motivate them to meet and do business. Execute the sequence after each marketing event.

If they don't schedule a meeting, send a sequence of a pre-drafted emails encouraging them to meet. If they still do not agree to meet, then add them to a long-term sequence. Use this general routine for referrals as well.

Short-term sequences are customized for specific triggering events and personalized to the individual. They can be used for prospect follow up as well as sales campaign follow-ups.

At the conclusion of the short-term sequence, if they have not taken action then move them into a long-term sequence.

Step 3. Implement long-term follow-up campaigns to nurture warm relationships and build credibility as a trusted resource. These are ongoing sequences. A contact stays in this campaign until they take action.

Long-term sequences are useful for prospects, clients, professional networks, and centers of influence. They allow the broadest flexibility in staying in touch. You can use any of the elements from the following Touch Points Menu.

Touch Points Menu

There are many ways to stay in touch. Emails and phone calls are just the most common. Consider these:

Face-to-face meeting	Telephone call
Email	Direct mail
Social media post	Dinner/lunch
Greeting card	Special event
Gift on special occasion	Text message

Email

Email is the most useful medium for staying in touch. It offers the most flexibility regarding content, reception, and response. You say what you want, when you want. The recipient is free to view it when they want and reply when they want.

You can send emails to individuals or to groups. Even group emails can be personalized when using the appropriate software so they appear to be individualized.

Look at using email marketing service providers to make it easy to send emails to large groups. Just create a document, and send to prospects, clients, or segments of either group. It makes it easy to stay in touch. Popular email service providers include Constant Contact, MailChimp, AWeber, and Infusionsoft.

Social Media

Social media applications such as Facebook, LinkedIn, Google Plus, and Twitter are the contemporary way to stay in touch. A vast majority of your clients and customers use these sites. They use them to communicate with people they know. Plus, more and more, they use them as tools for research. For example, when someone refers another person to me for whatever reason, I go online to Google, LinkedIn and Facebook to do basic research. That is what others are doing about you. In today's environment, you must have a social media presence in addition to a professional website.

Facebook

Business owners and professionals need a Facebook business page these days just as Yellow Page ads were needed in the past. Do you remember these? A Facebook business fan page is different than a personal profile and needs to be treated that way. Only professional content should be included.

A Facebook page features a main profile page and sub-pages, called tabs. In essence a Facebook fan page acts just like a mini website. Facebook pages should include your name, company name, contact information, what you do, and a link to your website. Always include an interesting, relevant image for the wide profile image. Similarly with the secondary Pages include relevant images.

People find your Facebook page through other promotions that direct them to the page. They must "Like" your page before they get on the distribution list to receive future posts from you. That is a big deal. Posts are the way you continue to stay in touch on Facebook.

How often do you make a post on Facebook? The school is still out on that. Some social media manager's advocate posting daily. Others say three to four times weekly. In the end it is your choice. Do not worry about being too bothersome. Studies show that only 16% of posts are viewed by fans due to the large volume of traffic on Facebook. If that is true, then don't worry about overburdening your viewers.

Show three to four useful resource-type posts that include a call to action offer to learn more. Then post one clear sales offer. Build your credibility as a valued resource.

Here are the essential parts of a Facebook post:

- Text content with interesting messages. Grab the reader's attention in a short paragraph.
- Image that is interesting and relevant. Catch the eye of the viewer as they scroll down the newsfeed. They will start on the image before they read text. Grab images from the Internet by searching a keyword in Google.
- End the post with a call-to-action that urges them to click a hyperlink that takes them where you want them to go. It is a waste of a post if you do not motivate them to take some action such as learn more about the topic and/or subscribe to your offer.

LinkedIn

LinkedIn is used mostly by business professionals and definitely not for casual entertainment viewing. Consequently it is used differently. LinkedIn is most useful for business-to-business networking. Build a LinkedIn page with an executive headshot not a casual photo taken with your iPhone. I am surprised at the number of profiles that lack a professional photo. In your profile in the space for your job title, write a professional headline that concisely states <u>what you do</u>, not your job title. Include company information, background information on your education, and previous employment. In the summary, describe how you help clients and what you are passionate about.

You can form groups with others by "Connecting" with them. Thereafter they will see your posts in their newsfeed. Make posts periodically, always including an interesting, relevant image to accompany the text. The image will catch their eye and draw attention to your message.

Summary

Staying in touch with prospects and clients is one of the cheapest forms of marketing. You establish warm relationships with prospects, nurture long term relations with clients, and achieve top-of-mind presence. When they are ready to do business, you will be the first one they think about when you have consistently performed the following actions.

- Build and maintain an email contact list
- Touch each contact every 7-14 days via the multiple channels
- Become a valued resource by way of useful information contacts
- Do something – don't wait

Practice 4

BOOST RECURRING REVENUE USING TYPE-V SERVICE

We have all seen commercials on TV of a woman running on an inclined treadmill with a narration of "to become better, to grow stronger, to be ready." The message is that an incline burns more energy than a level surface. Well, that's fine for physical fitness, but why would you do that in business? Why would you make it harder?

In essence, that is what business owners do by sticking with a transactional revenue model versus a recurring revenue model. The transactional model requires new sales to generate revenue. Those sales are not assured. It is characterized by inconsistent commission sales, ups and downs of income, and frantic surges in marketing. It all grows tiresome. Many small business professionals live in that exasperating world for years, never adopting a solution that could make their lives so much better.

On the flip side, a recurring revenue model levels the peaks and valleys. Fees and residual revenues flow in automatically without having to make a new sale. As long as the client relationship remains intact the recurring revenue continues. Recurring models grow more popular every year for big companies, small businesses, online enterprises and face-to-face businesses. A report by the independent research group, The Incyte Group revealed that 50% of companies had either adopted or were planning to adopt recurring revenue models.

Recurring revenue models create arrangements for continuous, recurring revenue based on an initial deliverable. It creates longer-term relationships with clients beyond the initial sale. We see examples all around us in many forms including online membership accounts, monthly fitness gym memberships, home HVAC maintenance contracts, legal services retainers and more. I did it in my practice with annual financial advisory fees. Many of these recurring revenue models incorporate auto-renewal features with a credit card versus mailing invoices.

Certain types of products deliver recurring fees after the original sale as long as the buyer pays the annual invoice. These include life insurance, auto, homeowners, long term care insurance and others. These arrangements have good retention from year to year because it is not easy to switch providers. Other products deliver recurring fees to the business as long as the client continues the relationship. These include investment products such as annuities, investment portfolio wrap accounts and others. The small fees are deducted from the investment account automatically.

Other services deliver a hybrid approach where revenue is recurring so long as the provider-client relationship remains strong, yet there are low barriers to switching. These include a hair stylist, tax preparer, favored auto mechanic, and others. There is no binding agreement, but the customer keeps returning periodically for the good service.

Benefits Of Recurring Revenue

Recurring revenue models have many advantages over transactional models. The biggest benefits are:

- Consistent, predictable income. The revenue arrives predictably on a regular basis in amounts that are assured and can be projected. It makes it easier for business planning. It flattens out the unevenness and reduces stress.

- Builds loyalty with clients. Clients remaining with a subscription program (periodically-renewing program) are demonstrating their trust and satisfaction with the service. As long as expectations are met – and exceeded – the revenue continues. People do not like change.

Most will remain loyal when their patronage is valued.

- Increases the value of the business. The fair market value of a business is a function of the of revenue it produces and how long the revenue continues. Recurring revenue models offer greater foresight into predictable cash flows and make it easier to predict future revenue growth. Potential buyers like this and will pay more for it.

Adopting A Recurring Revenue Model

Transforming your business from the traditional transaction-based model to a recurring revenue model is straight forward, but not easy. The general process is:

Step 1. Identify the product or service you are converting from the transaction model to the recurring model. This could be easy or complicated.

Step 2. Create a client re-engagement program to deliver extra value periodically in return for recurring fees. Define what you are going to do at each engagement opportunity. This sets expectations in the minds of clients and eliminates their worry of whether you might forget them. This differentiates you from many other competitors.

Step 3. Build the billing and collection system. This could take various forms ranging from invoicing, automatic bank drafts, or automatic credit card charges.

Any of these will work as long as someone is tasked with doing it. It is best when automated.

Step 4. Create a way to auto-renew the engagement. Find a way to avoid asking for another check. You do not want to face this every year, particularly if the fee is large. Maybe you chicken out or put it off for whatever reason. What if they say no? All these situations are avoided if it auto-renews, with the client's prior approval of course. That way the renewal happens whether or not you meet with the client. Remember, clients dislike writing checks as much as you dislike asking for them. When it gets billed automatically, they are comfortable with it. Believe me, I have witnessed it.

Step 5. Implement up-sell and cross-sell capabilities. Each time you interact with clients while delivering on the on-going service, you are presented with the opportunity to offer another service/product that may benefit them. Give them the opportunity to say "yes."

Make It Type-V Service

Make your recurring revenue program a Type-V service. Install recurring, value-added services that are pre-planned where the buyer knows what they will get and when they will get it. They will pay a recurring fee to be part of the service.

Type-V service does not have to be your only service. It can be your premium option to complement the other standard options. Offer it regardless of the type of business you are in. Give customers a choice. Promote it as your best overall value.

Clients want your advice and wisdom and they want to pay you for it.

Summary

If you are not already providing recurring revenue offerings in your business model then you have a huge opportunity in front of you. While it takes some effort to create and implement such offerings, it is well worth it. Recurring revenue is the business model of the future.

Practice 5

PREPARE TO TRANSITION WHILE YOU ARE GROWING

Just in case something unexpected may happen, start preparing now. We all will exit our businesses eventually whether it is through retirement, disability, personal reasons or even premature death. It may not happen soon, but we should prepare anyway. The number two habit of highly effective people, from Stephen R. Covey's book <u>The Seven Habits of Highly Effective People</u>, is "begin with the end in mind." In this case, begin structuring your business model right now to maximize its value so you are prepared to transition. Then when the time comes, your business has maximum value without you having to scramble making major adjustments at the last minute.

It is easier to grow your business using a model embodying recurring impact and encouraging repeat sales.

Such strategies make your business look more appealing to potential buyers who offer higher purchase prices. That eliminates any fire-sale scenarios in the event of an untimely, unplanned transition.

By implementing proper strategies that maximize fair market value you remove a significant stress point and accelerate the maturity of your business. It gives you freedom to move on to other things if you become tired of doing this any longer. You can walk away with more cash.

After all, what is a business really worth? What value does it have? A business is an entity that generates revenue in return for delivering products and services. The fair market value of a small business is a function of the amount of revenue it produces and how long the revenue continues.

Let's take a look at how to calculate the value a business and then examine the ways you can prepare to maximize that value in your own business.

How To Value A Business

Accurately valuing a small business is a challenging process for buyers and sellers. However, it doesn't have to be overwhelming. Valuation is more art than science. A seller is emotionally attached to the business and may factor in years of hard work and personal relationships with clients into the sales price. That seller wants the highest price possible. On the other hand, a buyer's view point is quite different. The buyer wants to pay the lowest price possible.

The challenge is achieving a fair balance between the seller and buyer, and formulating an accurate valuation. A fair balance is a win-win solution with both seller and buyer walking away with dignity and respect. Furthermore, if it is a personal services business like a financial services practice, make it a win-win-win solution where the clients are stakeholders in addition to the seller and buyer. Motivate the clients to be supportive of the transition.

Richard Parker, author of the book <u>How To Buy A Good Business At A Great Price</u>, provides the following excellent summary of the several methods to calculate the value of a business:

- Income Multiple Method: The selling price of a business is a product of the net income and a "multiple" (defined below).
- Rules Of Thumb Method: The selling price of other "like" (similar) businesses is used and adjusted by a multiple of cash flow or a percentage of revenue.
- Income Capitalization Method: The future income (based upon historical data and a variety of assumptions) is calculated and used to determine a selling price.
- Asset Valuations Method: Calculates the value of all of the assets of a business and arrives at an appropriate price.

The last three methods are generally not used for small businesses. Asset-based valuations do not work well for small business purchases because assets are used to generate revenue and nothing more. They are used to supplement other components of valuation. Income Capitalization Method is generally applicable to large businesses. It often utilizes a factor that is far too arbitrary. It is not useful for small businesses. The "Rule of Thumb" method may be too general since it's hard to find any two businesses that are exactly the same.

The Income Multiple Method is the way to go for small, personal services businesses. You have probably heard of businesses selling at "x times earnings." However, this can be quite subjective. When buying a small business, every buyer wants to know how much money they can expect to make from the business. Therefore, the most effective number to use as the basis of the calculation is what is known as total "Owner Benefits."

The Owner Benefits amount is the total dollars that the buyer can expect to extract or have available from the business based upon what the business has generated in the past.

The theory behind the Owner Benefit number is to take the business's profits, add the owner's salary, then add the benefits. The Owner Benefit formula is:

Profit (Pre-Tax) + Owner's Salary + Owner Perks

Then apply a "multiple" to this number to establish a valuation. That multiple is based upon a variety of factors.

What Multiple to Use?

Typically, small businesses sell in a one to three times multiple of this figure. Now, this is a wide range, so how do you determine what to apply?

Begin by understanding that a 1.0-times multiple is for those businesses where the seller is "the business." In other words: "as out the door goes the seller, so too can go the clients." Financial services practices, consulting businesses, professional service practices, and one-man businesses fall in this category. These practices may lack unique client service models that are transferrable to the new owner. They may lack things that bond clients to the practice.

A 1.5-to-2 times range may be applied to businesses that have recurring revenue from contractual arrangements with clients, residual fees from products, strong client service models with scheduled repeat engagements, and extensive routine staff involvement with clients. There are strong bonds that bind clients and their fees to the practice.

A 3.0-times multiple may be applied to businesses that have some proprietary item such as an exclusive territory, a growing industry, historical pattern of growth, and others. With these, the seller is not the most crucial factor.

Now the big question. What multiple applies to your Owner's Benefit number? Will it be 1, 2, or 3 times

Owner's Benefit? A strong case can be made for a higher multiple when there are "multiple-boosting factors" embedded in the business.

What Are Multiple-Boosting Factors?

The following factors affect the multiple used in valuing a business:

- Recurring revenue from repeat programs, contractual programs and subscription services.
- Residual fees from products.
- Strong client service model with scheduled repeat engagement opportunities for new business.
- Extensive, routine staff interaction with clients that strengthen relationships.
- Unique, proprietary programs benefiting clients that no one else offers.
- Primary value is in the services the clients get and not who delivers it.
- A Plan-B to continue operations if the owner is unable to work for a temporary period of time.

Now take a look at your current business model. What are you selling? Are most of your sales one-time transactions? Do you have programs that set the expectation for repeat interactions? Do your principal products or services require periodic renewal? Are your processes the primary value of the business or is it you personally? If the answer to the last three questions is no, then you have work to do.

What you have to do is build a YES-Strategy for recurring engagements. Each one strengthens the justification for applying a higher multiple to your selling price. Each one generates more current income and differentiates you from the competition.

Just in Case

Right now your business may be doing great and you have no plans to transition. Then something unexpected happens, you cannot work. What then?

It happened to a friend of mine, a financial advisor. He had a heart attack that put him in the hospital and home bed-rest for several months. He had capable staff to handle administrative matters, but no licensed person to make investment trades and give financial advice. Luckily, a friend and colleague in a separate office, yet affiliated with the same broker-dealer, was there to help. She came in and filled the void until he was back on the job. They worked out an income sharing arrangement under the supervision of the compliance manager.

As a result, when he was back in the office, they drafted a buy-sell agreement to define specifically what would happen in the event of a planned or unplanned event necessitating a transition. It identified the triggering reasons and the formula by which to establish the value of the business and the terms for buy-out. That was fortunate for his family because he died two years later.

You don't want that to happen to you. Begin now to identify who will come in to help keep the business operation going when you are out for health reasons. Establish a buy-sell agreement with someone now. You can always modify it later. Get something in place, just in case.

Insure The Risk

Consider covering the risk of financial hardship from a disability with Business Overhead Disability Insurance and funding the buy-out at death with Buy-Sell Life Insurance. They may prove to be life savers. While the premiums may be significant, the benefits are huge.

Summary

Your transition is going to happen sometime. Whether or not you are considering it now, it is important to install the Multiple-Boosting Strategies in your business. They will generate more current revenue and increase your equity in the business. Start getting ready now.

Part V

Breaking Down The Wall

Chapter 14

NOW THAT YOU KNOW

We have covered a lot of ground in our journey of discovery witnessing small business owners encounter obstacles stalling their progress. Generally it is where limited production systems slow down due to increased volume. Typically in these situations, the small business owner is involved in the mechanics of production. They are so wrapped up in the process, it is difficult for them to step back and evaluate how to unjam the system.

This happens in all types of businesses whether it is financial services, dry cleaners, restaurants, law firms, or lawn maintenance. It does not matter. Every business is a complex machine of moving gears, cogs, and levers. Sooner or later something jams. How do you unjam it? While individual businesses are unique, the general concepts for dealing with obstacles is the same.

In the previous chapters we examined special tools to loosen the gears and get them turning again. These tools are business practices to structure and manage the business for effective growth.

The first set of tools are the five practices in *The Business Breakout Blueprint*®.

Practice #1 Build a team and delegate. A practice that reduces stress, increases capacity, and focuses energy onto growing the enterprise.

Practice #2 Differentiate yourself with premium delivery. A practice that attracts ideal clients to services with unique value not delivered by other providers in the field.

Practice #3 Stay in touch with prospects and clients. A practice that keeps you top-of-mind so they think of you when they are ready to do business.

Practice #4 Boost recurring revenue with Type-V service. A practice that delivers high value service in exchange for recurring revenue.

Practice #5 Prepare to transition while you are growing. A practice that maximizes the value of your business so you can be ready to transition on your own terms.

The second tool is the *Continuous Engagement Model* which emphasizes re-engagement opportunities recognizing that it is five times easier to sell to an existing client than it is to sell to a prospect. It makes the notion of re-engagements an expectation in the minds of clients.

They welcome regular interactions that bring real value to them. You are provided regular opportunities to you to do more business.

The third tool is *Type-V service* which is pre-paid access to recurring, value-added services that are preplanned. The core concept is delivering additional value to clients on a regular basis and they pay a periodic fee to participate. They expect to receive real value because they are paying the recurring fee. In their minds it elevates the perceived quality of the service.

Armed with these powerful tools there are all kinds of ways to break down the wall that is holding you back. Learn more in the next chapter.

Chapter 15

BREAKTHROUGH FOREVER

Now that you are armed with the tools, how do you use them to break through your own walls? There will always be another wall. They arise from the complexities generated by current success.

You must take a step back, assess your frustrations, and apply the tools you have been given here. Here is a nine step process to do that.

1. Recognize it. Admit you have a problem.
2. Step back, identify the issues that bother you, big and small. Are they problems or annoyances?
3. Brainstorm these problems with someone you trust. Maybe that can help you see the real underlying issues.
4. Clarify your vision of where you wish to be in three years. Answer the R-Factor question. "If we were meeting three years from today - and you

were to look back over those three years - what has to have happened during that period for you to feel happy about your progress?"

5. List the positive opportunities that you hope to gain emotionally, financially, and professionally.

6. Identify the obstacles standing in the way of achieving this vision (physical things, issues, people, resources, capabilities).

7. Design strategies and tactics to move toward your vision. Use the tools in this book. Set measurable goals.

8. Establish a timeline and milestones to implement the strategies, tactics, and ultimately the vision.

9. Get started. Find someone to hold you accountable. Consider a coach.

Brainstorm your way through these nine steps using one of my other tools, the *Vision Strategy Quick Plan*. I created it to help me get my thoughts down easily without getting tied up in a formal structure. It is intended to get you off on a fast start focusing on what is important. Once you clearly see the destination, then it is easier to figure out how to get there. A copy is shown on the following pages.

As you do the planning to get out of your current rut to move to higher levels consider incorporating the practices from the *Business Breakout Blueprint*® into your business. They are proven to be effective and can be applied separately or together. For example, Practice #1 – Build a team and delegate – is a must-do for everyone. Practice #2 – Differentiate yourself with premium delivery – can be implemented together with Practice #4 – Boost recurring revenue with Type-V service. Also Practice #5 – Prepare to transition while you are growing – should be done along with Practice #4 and Practice #1. There are other useful combinations as well. They produce powerful, transformational results.

I will continue on my mission to spread the word through speaking and training to companies and groups.

If you want my help, simply contact me via email at the following address.

Email to: support@gethvc.com

Free tools at: www.gethighvalueclients.com

William A. Van Hoy
Get High Value Clients Growth Program
a DBA of Value Marketing Systems, LLC

Vision—Strategy Quick Plan

What: _____

Vision: Describe what you see as things work out perfectly.

Opportunities: Why is this important? What benefits can be achieved?

- ☐ _____
- ☐ _____

Obstacles: Standing in the way – including things, issues, people, uncertainties, fears

- ☐ _____
- ☐ _____
- ☐ _____

Strategies: Actions to pursue vision and deal with obstacles

- ☐ _____
- ☐ _____
- ☐ _____

Timing: Milestone and completion dates to do activities

- ☐ _____
- ☐ _____

Vision—Strategy Quick Plan

The Vision—Strategy Quick Plan focuses your attention on one thing you want to do. Use a separate template for each other area you want to achieve. It is designed for quick development.

Vision

Think ahead three years. You are doing exactly what you want to be doing and you are very happy with the ways things have turned out. Describe what is happening, what you are doing, and how you are feeling. Describe it so you can see it clearly.

Opportunities

Why is this important to you? What do you hope to gain emotionally, financially, and professionally? What benefits do you see for yourself?

Obstacles

What do you see standing in your way of achieving this vision? Is it time constraints? Is it financial related? Are there other people that may oppose or hinder you? Are you apprehensive about undertaking this? Do you feel you do not have enough knowledge and experience to undertake this? List all these things whether real, subjective, rational, or irrational.

Strategies

What actions can you pursue to move toward your vision and overcome the obstacles? Think through the steps of the process. Be specific as possible. Specify start and completion dates.

Timing

Summarize the timeline you envision that leads to ultimate success. Extract the dates and timing required of the various strategies defined above. Transfer these dates to your personal calendar.

ABOUT THE AUTHOR

William A. Van Hoy is the founder of *The Get High Value Clients Growth Program* and insightful advisor to small business owners. His passion is helping entrepreneurs break free of the obstacles holding them back and differentiate themselves to attract high value clients.

Bill has a background filled with varied interests including twenty-one years as business owner and Certified Financial Planner preceded by twenty-one years as a Surface Warfare Officer in the US Navy. His education includes certification as a CFP® from the College for Financial Planning, a Master's of Science in Command, Control and Communications from the Naval Postgraduate School, and a Bachelor's of Science in Electrical Engineering from North Carolina State University.

Bill is active in the community serving on the board of a professional business association, past-president of a non-profit youth shelter, and past-president of a community service association.

Bill's life mission includes enabling his family and friends to achieve the successes they want in life and making a positive difference in his part of the world.